STANISLAVSKI IN REHEARSAL

STANISLAVSKI
IN REHEARSAL

Vasili Torporkov

Translated by Jean Benedetti

METHUEN DRAMA

Reprinted with a new cover design 2008

First published by Methuen in Great Britain in 2001

1 3 5 7 9 10 8 6 4 2

Translation and Introduction copyright © Jean Benedetti, 2001

A CIP catalogue record for this book
is available from the British Library

ISBN 978-1-4081-0687-7

Methuen Drama
A & C Black Publishers Ltd
36 Soho Square
London W1D 3QY

www.acblack.com

Printed and bound in Great Britain by
CPI Cox & Wyman, Reading, RG1 8EX

Contents

Introduction

Vasili Toporkov's book, *Stanislavski in Rehearsal*, is one of the most valuable and accessible books on Stanislavski's personality and working method. It contains, the Conclusion apart, the minimum of theory and jargon, although inevitably certain key terms of the 'system' will be found, since they were in regular use during rehearsal.

Toporkov gives a vivid personal account of an eleven-year period during which he worked with Stanislavski. It is an almost blow-by-blow account of someone learning to come to terms with the 'system'. The authenticity of Toporkov's account is attested by the number of passages which are similar to pages in Stanislavski's own writings.

Toporkov was one of those rare people who were taken into the Moscow Art Theatre from the outside. Most of company were either founder members or graduates from the Moscow Art Theatre School and were familiar with Stanislavski's ideas, in one form or another.

Toporkov was twenty-eight when he joined the Moscow Art Theatre. He had graduated in St Petersburg in 1909 and he gives an illuminating account of the deficiencies of actor training even in the best schools. So it was that for eleven years, from 1927 to 1938, he rethought and relearned his craft.

He provides a multifaceted account of Stanislavski's personality – kind, humorous, demanding, pernickety, angry, ruthless, tyrannical, dedicated, desperate to pass on his legacy despite his illness. There was very little that was personal in Stanislavski's anger. It was only his concern for artistic perfection that made him intolerant. Nonetheless, he inspired intense personal loyalty and affection not least because he did not ask others to do what he had not, often with great difficulty, done. Old and frail as he was, when he had to, he could stand up and do it.

The core of Toporkov's book consists of accounts of the rehearsals for three productions: *The Embezzlers* (1928), *Dead Souls* (1932) and *Tartuffe* (1938). Because of his enormous workload, Stanislavski took a supervisory role in most productions. A director would be assigned to a play, and would rehearse it until the cast felt it was ready to show to Stanislavski. He would then revise, change and correct until he was happy.

The production of Kataev's *The Embezzlers* was part of Stanislavski's campaign to secure the position of the Moscow Art Theatre in the new Soviet Union. Although it had been defended by Lenin, it was seen by the hard left as a relic of a bygone era. One of the reasons for the European and American tours of 1923 and 1924 had been to remove the Moscow Art Theatre from the battlefield. Now Stanislavski had to demonstrate that it had a proper place in a new society and that the realism he advocated could be relevant to a new Soviet audience. He believed the 'system' was the best way to achieve performances that were both aesthetic and relevant. His determination to develop, apply and teach the 'system' increasingly, therefore, took on a moral and ethical character. He spared nobody, second-best was not good enough. It was into this situation that a largely unsuspecting Toporkov walked. This production was his baptism of fire and he recounts his struggles with great honesty.

There is then a three-year gap. *The Embezzlers* opened in April 1928 and in the autumn of that year Stanislavski suffered a heart attack that put an end to his acting career and altered the entire pattern of his life. Over the next ten years, both by choice and necessity, he turned away from directing to developing and teaching the 'system' and what came to be called the Method of Physical Action. He remained, however, until the mid 1930s very much in control of the artistic policy of the Moscow Art Theatre, defending it on the one hand against the party officials who wanted it to churn out more productions – 'pot-boilers' as he contemptuously called them – and the so-called avant-garde on the other, who reduced the actor to a mere cog in the wheel of a vast theatrical machine. Nowhere is this more clear than in his work on Bulgakov's adaptation of *Dead Souls*.

Sakhnovski was the nominal director for *Dead Souls*. Rehearsals were chaotic and were strung out over two years, mainly because of Stanislavski's illness. The play was not rehearsed in sequence but scenes were shown to Stanislavski as they were ready. The script went through three versions, and by the time Stanislavski had finished little was left of the original production, or the designs. He got rid of what he saw as the 'formalist' trappings of Sakhnovksi's staging, with its grandiose sets, and focused on the interplay, the psychology of the characters. In this he was doing precisely what Gogol had asked for in his notes for the original cast of *The Inspector General*: concentrate first on the way the characters feel and think, what drives them, and then think about their external behaviour and their costume. The production, rethought and redesigned by Stanislavski, received a mixed critical reception, but this was mainly due to the flaws in the script, which seemed little more than a string of small scenes with little dramatic growth. But Bulgakov's third version of the script provided excellent material for actors, which Stanislavski exploited to the full. It was precisely because the performances that Stanislavski drew from his cast were so real and vivid that *Dead Souls* remained in the repertoire well into the 1960s.

By the time Stanislavski came to work on *Tartuffe* he was extremely ill and housebound. He made it clear to the group of actors who came to Leontievski Lane that he was not interested in a finished production, only in applying the Method of Physical Action. He wanted to prove that it could be applied to a major classic play. Toporkov's account shows him using the same methods with seasoned professionals that he and his assistants were using with students at the Opera-Dramatic Studio, which are described in *Stanislavski and the Actor*.

Stanislavski died before work on the play was complete but he had done his essential work, which was to train a group of highly talented actors in the 'system' and the Method of Physical Action. The fact that they were able to implement his principles when working on the rest of the play, and to present a performance that all agreed was astonishing both for its quality and its innovation, vindicated Stanislavski's ideas.

Toporkov's book has a wider historical significance. Written between 1949 and 1950, it was the first description of Stanislavski at work. In his lifetime Stanislavski published only two works in the Soviet Union: *My Life in Art* (1926) and *An Actor's Work on Himself, Part One* (1938). The eight-volume edition of his *Collected Works* did not begin to appear until 1954 and *An Actor's Work on Himself, Part Two*, which had been published in a different version in the Unites States in 1950 as *Building a Character*, came out only in 1955.

Stanislavski's work was known only to a limited circle and was not universally accepted. There were those who considered the Method of Physical Action, with its emphasis on conflict and contradictions, as incompatible with the theory of socialist realism, which was precisely based on an absence of conflict. But it was Stalin who decided policy and Stalin who decided that the Moscow Art Theatre, *his* theatre, should become the model for all Soviet theatres and the 'system' the method for training actors and directors. He had destroyed the avant-garde, executed Meyerhold, silenced others. The fiction was that socialist realism, as it had been proclaimed since the 1934 writers' congress, was the direct descendant of Russian realism of the nineteenth century. Thus Stanislavski, who had been perceived as the natural heir to Gogol, Ostrovski, Shchepkin and the Maly Theatre since he was a young man, became a key figure. We can see the beginning of this process in the final paragraphs of Toporkov's book. They may appear a necessary nod in the direction of conformity, but since nothing could be published without the most rigorous censorship, we can assume that Toporkov's words represented the party line.

Finally, Toporkov's book had one unexpected spin-off. In 1955, Brecht, who had been hostile towards Stanislavski at first and then cautious in his endorsement, read a German translation which appeared in 1955. Previously, he had identified the Stanislavski 'system' with the emotionally self-indulgent acting he had encountered in the United States, where everything revolved around the actor's personality. *Stanislavski in Rehearsal* showed him a completely different Stanislavski, someone concerned with action, structure and meaning. He wrote to Toporkov describing the book as the best source he had on Stanislavski's working method. He had, in fact, been testing out aspects of the Method of Physical Action since 1953.

The translation of *Stanislavski in Rehearsal* is intended to complete a set of books which began with *Stanislavski: An Introduction* and continued with *Stanislavski and the Actor*. These three books, it is hoped, will provide a comprehensive overview, both practical and theoretical of the 'system' and the Method of Physical Action.

This translation is by no means literal. This is a book by an actor talking about acting, using the everyday language Russian artists used. I have tried, as far as possible, to use the language that English-speaking actors and directors use among themselves. There are signs, towards the end of the book, that the final pages were written in a hurry, and inadequately edited. Readers will find that sometimes the same ideas are repeated, slightly differently, in successive paragraphs. I have resisted the temptation to tidy up the material.

There are a small number of technical terms. These are all fully explained in *Stanislavski and the Actor*. One word, however, needs special mention: organic. This was a key word for Stanislavski in his later years. It has, unfortunately, taken on a very particular meaning in recent years. For Stanislavski it had nothing to do with food or drink. He used it in its original sense as relating to the human organism, its natural functioning. Organic is whatever is in accord with natural human processes. Acting is organic when it is based on normal physiological and psychological processes, not on artifice. As Stanislavski put it:

> These two techniques are different from each other, in the way that real plants in a nursery differ from artificial flowers made in a factory.

I would like to express my grateful thanks to Dr Victor Borovsky, the eminent theatre historian, who went through the draft translation line by line and made many valuable suggestions based on his profound knowledge of Russian theatre. He also has the advantage of having seen Toporkov act. Any errors, of course, are entirely my own.

Jean Benedetti, 2001

About the Author

I finished drama school in Petersburg in 1909 when I was twenty, full of self-confidence, convinced of my talent, my knowledge, my technical proficiency and boldly set out on the difficult path actors have to tread . . . took one step and faltered.

My naive, childish prattle about the theatre was soon drowned in the confident, loud professionalism of the actors in the company I joined immediately on graduation.[1] Ever since then I have known alternate moments of hope and disappointment. They have often led me to the brink of despair – something any actor who has spent a lifetime in the theatre knows.

There are those for whom the absence of precise knowledge, of a theoretical basis for acting seems quite normal and natural to the theatre, but it is a major cause of these excruciating creative crises.

Stanislavski shed light on many of the obscure aspects of the creative process, and rescued us from wandering aimlessly along unknown byways, showing us safer, truer paths towards the mastery of our art.

I had the good fortune to work and be guided by him first-hand.

When he was training an actor, Stanislavski not only provided him with his craft, but helped him develop spiritually in many ways, showing him how he could serve his art as a member of society. 'We must love the art in ourselves, not ourselves in art,' he used to say.

This kind of art, fully supported by the most advanced technique, with a mission to educate the people in the best ideas the modern world has to offer, was always Stanislavski's ideal.

Stanislavski's tremendous authority, his comprehensive knowledge of the actor's creative nature, gave him the right to conduct daring experiments with them. The very high demands he made led, ultimately, to simpler, easier solutions to the problem of physically embodying a character being found.

In honour of a great theatre teacher, conscious of the debt I owe him that can never be repaid, I have decided that the main aim of my life is to make his ideas known.

[1] The theatre, the Guardians of Public Temperance.

Every time I talk to young actors about technique, I feel the enormous interest they have in anything concerned with Stanislavski. This has led me to the idea of writing down the final occasions when I worked with this genius, and of discussing the newly discovered ways of creating a performance and a role, and thus smooth the path for our inquisitive young actors towards an understanding of Stanislavski's method.

The Journey Begins

I have trained as an actor twice in my life: the first time was at the Petersburg Imperial Theatre School, which was attached to the Aleksandrinski Theatre (1906–1909), and the second time when I worked with Stanislavski at the Moscow Art Theatre (1927–1938).

When I look back at my first period of study, and compare it with what I learned from Stanislavski, I am more and more convinced that all the education I received at the Petersburg school did, for all its good points at the time, was to put an official piece of paper in my hand, acknowledging the fact that I had completed my studies. My work with Stanislavski, on the other hand, gave me a real chance to understand the basics of acting.

In this regard, it is of more than a little interest to recall the state which theatre schools were in before Stanislavski created his system. This little detour is not difficult for me since, as I have said, I studied theatre in a 'pre-reform' school, when Stanislavski was only just beginning his experiments to discover the theoretical basis of acting, and when his opinions carried very little weight in this field, especially for those of us in Petersburg.

The teacher of undisputed authority at the Imperial Theatre School in Petersburg was Davydov,[1] a famous actor at the Aleksandrinski theatre. He was the white-haired father figure. It was considered very good luck to be one of his pupils. His students adored him and obeyed him without question. Discipline in his classes was exemplary. On many occasions I was present not only as an observer but rehearsed plays with his pupils. At the time that made a great impression on me and, indeed, his classes were of genuine interest.

When he came into the rehearsal room, this venerable artist gathered the young students round him and gave inspiring speeches about the theatre, great Russian actors and the eminent Italian actor Tommaso Salvini whom he valued highly and skilfully imitated. Then he turned to the play that was to be rehearsed, told each actor where his abilities lay and where they

[1] Vladimir Nikolaevich Davydov (1849–1925)

didn't. He talked about the play itself and each character in detail. It was all very persuasive, clear and easy to understand. The students would rush on to the stage and start rehearsing, only to realise that they could not do what had seemed so simple, clear and easy a moment before. Their technique was inadequate. They couldn't achieve even a hundredth of what their beloved teacher had so clearly explained to them, and the more vivid his words, the more helpless and useless they felt. The stage exuded boredom, flatness and despair. The great master either fell asleep during his pupils' monotonous performance of a cheerful comedy, or burst out angrily, lambasting each actor in turn, giving devastating caricatures of their acting. Then, despite his advanced years and fatness, he would run on to the stage, like a young man, and give a brilliant performance of all the parts, then cheerfully go back to his seat to the applause of his flock and happily proclaim: 'Was that me or the devil incarnate?'[1]

Basking in his success, he was soon in a good mood and would end the class with funny stories or a demonstration of conjuring tricks at which he was quite remarkable. He recommended his pupils to study the art of conjuring, 'An actor should be able to do everything, act, sing, dance and do tricks'.

This great actor's personal charm, his penetrating, persuasive comments, his demonstration of his own professional skill, his fatherly concern for his pupils, which extended beyond the confines of the school, could not but have an enormous influence on future young actors in the development of their talent. Teachers like Davydov lovingly introduced the style of realistic acting that had been created by Shchepkin[2] and which flourished in the theatre at that time. It could be seen in the work of a galaxy of great actors both in Moscow and Petersburg, and in theatre academies. Under Davydov's influence his pupils began to look quite different from provincial, self-taught actors.

Other teachers of the period had their own individual qualities, their own skill in training young actors, but they all lacked one thing: a firm theoretical base and a coherent teaching method. What looked systematic at the time was, in comparison with the

[1] One of his favourite expressions.
[2] Mikhail Semionovich Shchepkin (1788–1863), friend of Pushkin and Gogol, leading actor at the Maly Theatre from 1830 until his death. Stanislavski took him as his model.

concrete, practical work Stanislavski did subsequently, more like running around in circles.

But, of course, I had studied in Petersburg, and only knew about the teaching there. Perhaps things were different in Moscow? I had never been to Moscow and had never attended classes by teachers like Lenski[1] and Sadovski[2]. From what I gathered from their pupils, who spoke of them with great respect, things were much the same there.

Of course, Lenski and Davydov trained a whole succession of actors of whom we are justly proud. It could not have been otherwise. Yet the future development of acting as an art required in its turn an improvement in teaching methods. Stanislavski managed to reveal many of the 'secrets' of acting technique, which great actors knew but could not explain to their pupils, although they tried to do so with all their heart and soul.

Stepan Yakovlev, an actor at the Aleksandrinski Theatre, in whose class I completed my studies, was somewhat different from his colleagues. Having trained under Davydov, he went to Moscow to work with Aleksandr Fedotov.[3] On his return to Petersburg, he brought back ideas about the teaching of acting that were new at the time, and which to some degree determined his future development.

Yakovlev's teaching method was much more progressive than Davydov's, and there was a different atmosphere in his classes which I became aware of since I was working simultaneously with Davydov. When Davydov took over the classes of his former student, because of his illness, we young people, for all our respect and admiration for a great actor, became somewhat critical of his old-fashioned methods.

In what sense was Yakovlev's teaching method rather more progressive? In those days the art of declamation – melodramatic declamation – flourished and tribute was paid to it in theatre schools. In the first half of the first year, instead of basic, specialist subjects, students learned 'recitation' which bore no relation to what actors actually do on stage. They studied almost nothing

[1] Aleksandr Pavlovich Lenski (1847–1908), an actor of great subtlety and refinement whom Stanislavski admired.
[2] Mikail Provovich Sadovski (1847–1910), a leading actor at the Maly Theatre. Taught by Shchepkin, he specialised in the works of Ostrovski.
[3] Aleksandr Filipovich Fedotov (1841–1895) was one of Stanislavski's early teachers, particularly at the Society of Art and Literature.

about that. Three-quarters of the year were spent in studies that were either useless or even, to some degree, harmful to them as actors. Very often pupils who were successful in declaiming found they were either poorly or totally unprepared when they turned to real acting.

Yakovlev introduced basic changes into first-year studies and steered them in a more appropriate direction. In his very first class he defined the difference between recitation and acting. He never taught declamation or even thought of doing so. He thought about reading extracts from works of literature in a different way, as a preparation for acting, or, to use a more modern expression, as exercises in verbal action. I won't go into details, as we shall encounter this idea many times later. While Yakovlev's teaching followed these lines, everything was fine and the students progressed well, taking their first, real steps. But after he had worked on literary extracts for a certain period of time, he would suddenly give up what is a wholly necessary and useful exercise, which students need to practise right to the end of their training, and set off on a completely wrong path.

Being spontaneous by nature and capable of deep feelings (and that was how he thought of acting), he was very demanding with his pupils when he approached the question of emotion in his classes. But what was easy for the highly talented Yakovlev was not always so for his students. It was clear that he never had to think where his emotion came from, or how to endow his characters with feeling. He didn't need a 'springboard'. He only needed to want something and it happened. It was another matter for his twenty-odd pupils, each with their own individual personality, mind and habits. Yakovlev knew nothing of the tortuous paths by which an actor achieves genuine emotion, genuine organic feeling, those 'gateways' through which you can arrive at your destination more securely, and which Stanislavski later discovered.

Yakovlev turned from the correct path he had followed in the first semester, and went down the forbidden path of trying to force feeling. Once he had finished with literary extracts of a descriptive nature, he gave his students emotionally charged works or speeches, such as 'On the Death of a Poet' by Lermontov, or Chatski's[1] final speech or a speech by the false Dmitri[2] or other

[1] Chatski is the leading character in Griboedov's *Woe from Wit*.
[2] In Pushkin's *Boris Godunov*.

things of that sort, and all he wanted was for the reading to be full of energy and great feeling. If he didn't get what he wanted, it was, as he put it, 'blah-blah-blah'. He didn't give us any real help and he wouldn't accept any excuses.

'I'm really not in the mood today. I can't find any feelings at all.'

'That's not my concern,' he would answer. 'There must be feeling. Read this poem and shed tears.'

'But I haven't any!'

'Then go and borrow something from Volkov-Semionov.' (That's what we called the theatre library where we borrowed playtexts.)

In Yakovlev's mind there was no doubt that an actor must have high energy and feeling, and if there were none at a given moment, then the actor had to pump himself up to get them, repeating the unsuccessful speech, scene or poem over and over again. He had a special way of coaxing an actor. He would bang his foot on the floor during the rehearsal so as not to interrupt the flow. It would have been better to stop the actor who was 'tearing a passion to tatters', calm him down and lead him through a succession of thoughts, images, apply other techniques which Stanislavski used in his work to arouse living, genuine feelings in his pupils.

Following Yakovlev's example, his pupils, individually and collectively, dutifully worked on their emotional energy, they bellowed furiously in every conceivable way such heroic lines as, 'Almighty God, Thou art my witness!', 'He is here, you hypocrite!', 'No, that is too much!', 'You lie, Rabbi!' When they spoke these and similar lines, the young students, unfortunately, did not see with their 'inner eye' the images contained in these lines, only their enthusiastically foot-tapping idol, Yakovlev.

Yakovlev made one of his favourite female students, who had a great gift for heroic roles, read at every class during the three years of her study a speech of Joan of Arc's,[1] trying to arouse a heroic sense of feeling in her. But neither a glittering account of how Ermolova[2] spoke the speech, nor his energetic, endless foot-banging was of any help. The young actress's emotional resources were not released, and if there was the occasional spark it was not

[1] In Schiller's *Maid of Orleans*.
[2] Marya Nikolaevna Ermlova (1853–1928), leading actress at the Maly Theatre, greatly admired by Stanislavski for his success is great heroic roles.

the result of Yakovlev's method but in spite of it. It was impossible to hold on to any feeling. It went as quickly as it had come. To hold on to it, you need to know how genuine feeling can be reached. Unfortunately, Yakovlev lacked that knowledge.

When he began rehearsal on the stage proper, Yakovlev's teaching methods again wavered between the good and the bad. He rejected, on principle, any direct demonstration of how to play this or that role. He was steadfast in applying it. Never once in three years of study did he go up on stage to show his pupils what to do, as his teacher Davydov often did. And he also, if somewhat vaguely, understood the importance of small physical actions and drew our attention to them, although he could not see in them the embryo of a future method. 'If you are portraying real life, everything you do on stage – drinking tea, peeling potatoes and so on – must conform to reality,' he said.

Yakovlev cannot be accused of leading his students directly to the result, to the portrayal of an external image, and away from the true path taught by Stanislavski: to start from one's own nature, from one's own feelings and your personal expression of them in the given circumstances of the play. He did that, but it was all brought to nothing by the teaching methods he used. Yakovlev talked about all the right things I have mentioned, and, to some degree, applied them in practice, but then contradicted himself by bowing to utilitarian considerations.

'I am making actors out of you. Most of you will go and work in the provinces. Out there you will create a role in two or three rehearsals. You have to be prepared for that. So, above all, you need practical skills. Here in the school, we will prepare a production in two weeks. When you leave, you will have a repertoire and expertise.'

What kind of expertise? For routine performances. But to some extent Yakovlev was right. Provincial theatres required actors with a wide repertoire, who could work fast and adapt to all circumstances. And how many were lucky enough, once they had finished their studies, to get engagements in good theatres in the capital?

The period of actor training was three years. That was considered adequate. Any hopes of further development were dependent on real work in the professional theatre. That view was the result of a limited knowledge of the actor's art.

But, while I speak of the inadequacy of old methods of teaching,

I don't wish to belittle the importance of theatre schools of the period for the growth of our theatrical culture, or, even less, to denigrate their teachers, who were great artists of the Russian stage. Many outstanding actors – Davydov, Yuriev, Petrovski, Ozarovski, Sanin and finally my own teacher Yakovlev – did important work in actor training. They all valued drama schools, loved them, and gave them all their strength without thought of personal gain, receiving scant sympathy from the majority of actors of the time who took an entirely negative view of such schools. I deliberately draw attention to the failings of their methods of teaching from the standpoint of contemporary knowledge, so as to define more precisely the truly great leap forward made by Stanislavski. With his genius, in his experiments, he built upon the wealth of experience of the best representatives of Russian realism's traditions in the theatre.

The art of directing was just making its first faltering attempts to move from simple stage management to something more creative. Yuri Yuriev, in his memoirs, describes an incident that occurred at the Aleksandrinski Theatre during rehearsals for Ostrovski's *Burning Heart*. Davydov broke traditional rehearsal methods by interrupting the session and correcting one of his pupils who was involved in the scene. The scene was not working and in his attempts to get it right Davydov asked for it to be done over and over again, much to the indignation of the other actors. 'This is not a school,' they told him. And this to someone who possessed great authority in the company, and was the pride of the Russian stage. So what could an ordinary director do, surrounded by this assembly of the great?

At that time rumours were circulating about Stanislavski's 'bizarre methods' at the Moscow Art Theatre. They were both contradictory and vague. Some said that Stanislavski was turning his actors into puppets, and/or into trained monkeys who, as the victims of his despotic will, merely carried out their master's instructions. Some, on the other hand, said that when he was rehearsing he sometimes asked the actors to improvise, without giving any precise moves or staging or using any of the other standard procedures. Then we heard the incredible rumour that when Stanislavski was working with the actor Uralov on the role of the mayor in Gogol's *Inspector General*, he rehearsed a scene, 'The

Mayor at the Bazaar', which is neither in the final play nor any of its drafts.

Actors from the Moscow Art Theatre would sometimes appear with actors from other theatres and they were already parading their special style, their special understanding of acting, their grasp of a special, mysterious working terminology, their special approach to creating a role. These innovations were all too bold, they challenged tradition. Stanislavski's 'bizarre methods' provoked a strong reaction from the company at the Aleksandrinski.

An interesting incident comes to mind. Uralov came to the Aleksandrinski in Petersburg from the Moscow Art Theatre. And since, in Moscow, he had played the mayor in *The Inspector General*, he alternated the role with Davydov. Once, during a break in rehearsal, Uralov respectfully turned to Davydov with a question about acting. The following dialogue ensued:

'Tell me, Vladimir Nikolaevich, in the first act, on your entrance to the officials, what do you bring on with you?'

'What do you mean, bring on with me?' Davydov replied, as though he had not understood.

'What state of mind are you in, what are your feelings, what is your intention? At the Moscow Art Theatre we have been taught . . .' (There followed a long explanation about different tasks, the given circumstances, etc.)

Davydov listened patiently for a while, containing his anger and contempt, and then interrupted Uralov with this sarcastic reply: 'I don't know what you bring on with you at the Moscow Art Theatre, but I bring on the idea that I am on the stage of the imperial theatre to play Gogol and *I* bring on Vladimir Nikolaevich Davydov with me, and not the devil incarnate!'

With that he turned away, indicating that the conversation was over.

This was spoken, of course, in anger and irritation against a smart alec, who was trying to be cleverer than the celebrated Davydov, a master of his craft, who not only had a well-deserved reputation for his talent, but was someone who could reflect on and analyse a role, someone who explored the subtleties of acting, and could create a well-rounded, polished performance. And yet, when he made is first entrance in *The Inspector General*, there was no trace of the self-satisfaction with which he had spoken to Uralov. On the contrary, his entrance as the mayor amazed us by the subtle, expressive logic of his behaviour as a frightened bureaucrat, fearful of official trouble. You only had to look to see what the mayor 'came on with'. But how this great actor achieved his results was a complete mystery to us. It was to this mystery that Stanislavski, the great reformer, later turned his penetrating eye.

Rumours which reached me in Petersburg about Stanislavski's work at the Moscow Art Theatre interested me, in the first instance, as it did others, only because it was unusual, not to say curious. But thinking over it later, and analysing his ideas more carefully, I felt that there must be an element of truth in them. The first tour of the Moscow Art Theatre that I saw in Petersburg, particularly the production of *The Cherry Orchard* (which was also being done at the Aleksandrinski), finally convinced me this was the case. I was overwhelmed by its remarkable artistic quality, which clearly underlined how out of date my former idol, the Aleksandrinksi Theatre, was. Bringing together the best representatives of the imperial theatre (Davydov, Dalmatov, Varlamov, Michurina, Yakovlev) on the same stage could not compete with the harmonious ensemble of their Moscow colleagues, which was not full of illustrious names, but was guided by the will of its innovative director.

This performance sealed my fate. All my thoughts were directed towards this new theatre, to a new kind of acting. I started to look for ways of getting near to Stanislavski. My dream only came true twenty years later. This gap was not without its uses. I worked a great deal in Petersburg and Moscow and in the provinces, playing many parts, gaining experience. I was successful, particularly in later years at the former Korsh[1] Theatre, before I entered the Moscow Art Theatre, and I learned much because I met talented, experienced actors and directors. All that might provide material for my memoirs, but I turn instead to my present book.

[1] Fiodor Adamovich Korsh (1852–1923) ran the most successful commercial theatre in Moscow.

The Embezzlers

Long, hard work is needed to educate an actor in the ethos and advanced technique of the Moscow Art Theatre. While he is learning, the actor also needs to be protected from harmful extraneous influences, and that is why so few 'outsiders' were ever invited in. Actors, as Stanislavski put it, must be 'nurtured' inside the theatre. The invitation I received to join the Moscow Art Theatre was one of those rare exceptions which the theatre's managers, for various reasons, sometimes made.

As I have already said, I joined the Moscow Art Theatre company with almost twenty years work behind me as an actor. Up till then, Stanislavski had never seen me on stage or off it, and decided to invite me into the theatre on the recommendation of colleagues running the theatre with him at the time, and whose judgement he had no reason to mistrust. But the final decision was considerably delayed as Stanislavski considered the entry of an actor into the Moscow Art Theatre a matter of the highest importance.

The first hint of a forthcoming invitation came two years before the actual event. Stanislavski considered the matter from all sides, making enquiries in different places and to different people, not only about me as an actor but as a person, a family man, a citizen, etc. And finally, when our first meeting took place[1] in his office at the theatre, we were both so nervous that we tried to sit in the same chair. I felt his piercing gaze on me, like someone acquiring a new piece for his collection, afraid of making the wrong choice.

Stanislavski's concern with establishing and teaching a new technique of acting was so deep that it began to take precedence over everything else he did in the theatre, especially in the last years of his life. And so, it was of particular interest to him to meet actors from other theatres, and try to bring them round to his way of thinking. For my part, I had dreamed for so long of meeting this great artist, and was desperate to learn from him, first-hand, the wonderful, new – but still rather vague – things I had heard

[1] March 1927.

about his kind of acting, by word of mouth in theatrical circles. This mutual interest of teacher and pupil did not abate when we worked together later.

After our first meeting, about which I can say little more, we met again in the study of his home in Leontievski Lane, where I experienced the excitement, the joy, the fear, the doubt, the hope that every actor who crossed his threshold always felt.

The second meeting was quite long – two, three, four hours – and took place in a homely atmosphere, which evidently had been specially arranged for our talk. On the table were bowls of nuts, sweets and fruit which Stanislavski offered me. We talked, of course, about the theatre. He questioned me carefully about what I liked. Which of all the parts I had played did I prefer, and why? What would I like to play? What would please me most, to join the Art or some other theatre? In other words, all the questions which nowadays, following his example, a theatre director would ask of a new actor he was taking into his company. But at that time it was something new, and the enormous number of questions, and the care with which Stanislavski put them, made a great impression on me. Stanislavski wanted detailed answers from me. He listened to them attentively and told me where my answers differed from his.

Our conversation was highly significant and instructive. But, unfortunately, I was so excited that I did not record this meeting in any detail immediately after, and now, after so many years, it is difficult to reconstruct it without distorting the truth. So, I leave it to one side. All I will say is that I was truly amazed by the way he treated me during that meeting. What struck me most was the extraordinary interest he took in anything and everything to do with the theatre. There was not a single detail that was not worthy of attention. I was acutely aware of the interest he took in all my answers, in every sentence I uttered, although he took care to hide it and tried to make our discussion seem casual, like an ordinary conversation. He did not always succeed. When I started to praise a certain highly successful production in Moscow (I knew Stanislavski had seen it), I suddenly saw such horror in his eyes that I had to stop mid-sentence. Only after many years did I realise how inept I had been. Stanislavski inveighed against that theatre and its director, first angrily then sarcastically, revealing the inadequacy of the thinking that lay behind the production, and then, unexpectedly, characterised its nature in one single, highly expressive gesture. I could not stop myself from laughing and that seemed to calm him somewhat.

But on the whole we had a quiet and wonderful conversation. At one point Stanislavski asked me a question but I had no time to answer as he was called to the telephone. He excused himself, and went to the telephone which was nearby. The call was from the theatre. I could hear the conversation quite clearly. It was about some quite minor matter, but he spent at least an hour heatedly trying to reach a decision on a matter of principle, taking no notice of the fact that the caller at the other end was agreeing with him. He was trying to establish a principle that would be valid for similar decisions in the future. He was so upset by this conversation that when he sat down he looked at me for a while with angry eyes, taking me for his caller, and when I timidly tried to answer the question he had put to me an hour before, he yelled fiercely, 'That's got nothing to do with it!' Then slowly he pulled himself together and our conversation continued. I tried to leave several times, fearful of taking up too much of his time, but he wouldn't let me. Finally our discussion came to an end. Taking me along the corridor to his front door, Stanislavski was kind and very attentive.

Stanislavski's attitude to me during my visit, his profound insights into acting, his unbounded dedication to theatre made an impression on me that it is difficult for me now to describe, but nothing in my whole life in the profession has ever been more powerful. The creative atmosphere he had established in the theatre, the whole style and character of the work, the relationships among the members of the company, which I witnessed, reinforced this impression, and I suddenly felt, as never before, the importance of what was happening in my life. I knew I was on the threshold of something new, unknown, exciting, that I had done something much more significant than just move from one theatre to another.

My artistic career at the Moscow Art Theatre started with a success. Stanislavski's colleagues were preparing to show him a roughly rehearsed production of Kataev's *The Embezzlers*.[1] There were still a few days to go before the presentation and there was still one small part to be cast. Sudakov, the director of the play, suggested I do it. It was character part, a comic role, and I was not worried by the fact I had only two or three rehearsals to prepare it.

[1] Opened 20 April 1928.

I was used to that. My appearance in this role was so successful that Stanislavski decided to give me one of the lead parts in the play – the cashier, Vanechka – that Khlemev had been rehearsing. He would be given my role. This was an important indication of Stanislavski's opinion of me. I was in seventh heaven. From now on everything will go like clockwork, I thought, and my fear of the difficulties involved in acting at the Moscow Art Theatre seemed no more than a figment of my imagination. So, in the autumn, after the summer break, we began to rehearse *The Embezzlers* again. And I was to play the cashier, Vanechka.

The play, which had been adapted from a short story, was loose in its construction. It was more like a revue sketch. The accountant, Filip Stepanovich, and the cashier, Vanechka, accidentally embezzle a large sum of money and are soon knee-deep in crime and new ventures. Having squandered the entire sum, they have to go back home and confess their crime to the police. In the course of the play, they become embroiled in both starkly dramatic and comic situations, which provided good material for 'acting'.

As a standard character type in the old sense, Vanechka is a simpleton, the kind of role I had learned to play at drama school. I set to work with great excitement. But this was not the kind of bit part I was used to creating on my own, and in which I had successfully made my debut. Vanechka appears right through the play and must blend in with the other characters and the overall style of the production. I was in trouble. When I was playing at the Korsh Theatre, no one ever said that my style was so very different from that of the Moscow Art Theatre. On the contrary, my proximity to their style was the reason for my being invited there. Nonetheless, when the need inevitably came to blend with the director and the other actors, there were problems and rough moments. I even tried to give up the role. But, finally, everything seemed to fall into place, and the play was ready for Stanislavski to see. The day came.

The presentation took place not on stage but in the foyer of the theatre. This was something new for me; the audience was almost under my nose, and what an audience! The cast played scene after scene in indications of sets. The performance was sketchy. It was more an outline of their roles than the real thing. I was not used to that but, all the same, I surmounted all the difficulties, and got through my first presentation quite successfully. Stanislavski was pleased with my performance and generally satisfied with what he had seen. I assumed that the opening of the show was only a matter of time and that, in any case, the worst problems were over, and that my way was open to the Moscow Art stage and the Moscow Art theatregoers. It was just a matter of polishing my performance. But that would come from contact with a live audience. How wrong I was! The really hard work only began when Stanislavski started to rehearse. Everything we had done up to then was just a rough sketch.

Stanislavski's rehearsals for this play were fraught with tension and anxiety. Things clearly weren't going well. Even the old hands at the Moscow Art Theatre were in trouble, and for the newcomers, who received the bulk of his attention, it was sheer murder. But my compensation was to see, for the first time, wonders of which, previously, I had no inkling, and which were being worked right there in front of me. I left every rehearsal enriched and disheartened. A new theatrical language, and new, totally unfamiliar methods of working bewildered me, inhibited me. I was an experienced actor but I felt like a bull in a china shop.

The first rehearsal took place in the so-called CO room. CO is an abbreviation of 'comic opera'. Nemirovich-Danchenko had once used this room to rehearse 'Mademoiselle Angot'. The name which it had been given at that time had stuck. We rehearsed 'at the table' – no moves. Stanislavski talked to us, cursorily went through some scenes, asked us questions and offered one or two comments.

Rehearsals 'at the table' were an innovation of the Moscow Art Theatre, which Stanislavski sometimes modified but he never denied their value. In old provincial theatres, and in the capital too, the only rehearsal at the table was the first read-through, when the script was gone through and cuts made. The next day, on stage, script in hand, the actors would go right through the play from beginning to end. The moves were set at the first rehearsal, then the cast rehearsed 'off the book', with every actor trying to find the 'right tone' for his part, then there was a full dress rehearsal, in costume and make-up, and then came the performance with everyone acting as best they could, at his own peril.

The directors of the Moscow Art Theatre had set themselves much more difficult tasks and so, of course, they had to find better ways of rehearsing, one of which was rehearsals 'at the table', where the cast, under the director, would carefully analyse every section of the play, and even, at this stage, look for ways of playing them. Stanislavski suggested I play one of my scenes. Finding myself in an unusual situation, with no moves to help me, face to face with Stanislavski, I wasn't sure what to do, but a certain theatrical experience boosted my self-confidence and I soon fell into the 'right tone' which I had worked out in previous rehearsals. I more or less did what I had done the first time we showed the play to Stanislavski but, contrary to my expectations, I didn't see a hint of approval on his face. Having watched the scene, he was silent, then he coughed and with a polite smile said:

'Excuse me, but you're using a certain "tone" . . .'

'How so?'

'You're trying to play the part with a certain "tone" which you have already worked out.'

I didn't know what he was talking about. What else was I supposed to do? Of course there was a 'tone'. I had given a great deal of thought to it. After all, he had liked what I had done at the presentation! What was going on? I told him I didn't understand what he meant. Stanislavski explained that the most valuable thing in acting is to be able to find a living person in every part, to find oneself.

'You've saddled yourself with something you have worked out in your head, and it's preventing you from responding to what's going on around you as a living person. You're playing a character type and not a living human being.'

'Yes, but how . . . ?'

'Tell me, what's in your office?'

'I don't understand . . .'

'You're a cashier, so what's in your office?'

'Money . . .'

'Yes, money. And then what? Give me more details. You say, money. Fine, how much? What money? What kind? Where do you keep it? What kind of desk do you have, what kind of chair, how many lamps are there . . . ? Well, tell me how you run things.'

I said nothing for a long time. He patiently waited for my answer. I finally realised and said that I couldn't answer a single one of his questions, and I wasn't sure why I should know all this. Ignoring my last remark, he suggested I should think for a while and then answer just one of his questions. I said nothing.

'You see, you don't know what's most essential about your character, his daily work. What he lives for, what his concerns are . . .

'Here we have the cashier, Vanechka, a mild, modest young man. His office is his home. It is his holy of holies. It is the best thing in his life. Everything about it reveals the nature of his concerns: the cleanliness of the place, the order in which all the things he needs for his daily work are arranged, from the large, steel safe to his nice red and blue pencil, which he considers his best friend and calls Konstantin Sidorovich, and the electric lamp which he keeps so spotless that it seems the brightest source of light in the department. It is his pride. The locks of the fireproof safe are well greased and open and shut easily, without a hitch. The delightful way they click is beautiful, it is music to his ears. Packets of banknotes are ranged on the shelves inside. There are bills of a hundred, thousand, ten thousand, a hundred thousand. Vanechka can always tell you how much is in there at any given moment. He loves the actual process of paying in and paying out. Issuing and checking money in the department is a holy ritual, a work of art for him. It is a tragedy for him, as for the recipients, when he can't pay out because there is no money. Vanechka never makes mistakes, his accuracy is legendary. For all his youth and modesty, in his way he is famous in the world of accountancy, and nothing gives him more pride than his renown.

'The chief accountant is very fond of him. Vanechka, on his side, worships him as a soldier in the ranks might worship a great general. The slightest disturbance in Vanechka's world shakes him to the core. What if (God forbid) his boss were suddenly no longer at his desk? Or if there were fly specks on the light bulb? Or one of the clerks didn't sign the ledger on the proper line? These are the kind of workaday irritations Vanechka can talk about endlessly in his free time. It would be terrible to think what would happen if some financial error should creep in, or if a bundle of notes were one or two short. Such things have actually never happened to him. He only sees them in his nightmares.

'So, imagine how Vanechka feels when, after a series of devilish events, having drunk himself senseless, he wakes up on a train, in a sleeping car, on his way to Leningrad, and discovers 100,000 roubles he has embezzled, with the chief accountant lost in a drunken stupor and a strumpet in the upper bunk.

'This is utter madness, the monstrous destruction of his world, a tragedy! But you didn't create this world, you didn't experience it inside, you didn't try to bring it to life on stage. It doesn't matter if the writer hasn't shown it. But did you, when you were alone in your office, with the window shut so no one could see you, during the action, or before rehearsals began, in your own small corner, actually live through your character's little actions: dusting, cleaning the lamp, putting notes into piles, sharpening pencils, etc., etc.? At best you were trying to find ways of saying the dialogue, how you would deliver your first line, when you open the window to your office, when the part of your role the audience can see begins. You didn't put down the roots through which to feed your role.'

That is the gist of what Stanislavski said to me in rehearsal. I realised the profound truth of his words, but I had absolutely no idea how to put them into practice. How was I to rehearse? I tried to argue, I demonstrated another possible method of working, I spoke of my earlier successes, but all my arguments were easily demolished by Stanislavski's logic.

'I've played a few roles very well.'

'That's quite possible. But do you want to improve your acting?'

'That goes without saying.'

'I'll show you how to do that. And I want to spare you useless muddle, which is always painful, if you go off on the wrong track when you're working on a role.'

I wouldn't give in but kept on challenging him. With a sigh, Stanislavski said:

'Our new friend certainly knows how to argue!'

So, the rehearsal ended, bogged down in my first scene. Such a 'waste' of time seemed, as I remember, astounding. At the Korsh Theatre, we would have gone through the whole play. But the ideas Stanislavski had planted in my head took an amazing hold of me, they gestated until the next rehearsal, from which Stanislavski was absent, when we had a token set and props. I tried to do everything he had suggested, rather shame-faced, but it was all so new to me that I went red every time someone started watching me.

No, it all seemed like a devilish conspiracy! In the old days, everything had been so easy: you had the moves, the other actors, your cues, so start acting, but now . . . But still, I had to try again. Looking around me once more, I started dusting, sharpening pencils, tidying up. But no, that wasn't it. I was doing all this before the rehearsal, which hadn't begun yet. But the full sets were there.

So, let's try again, but absolutely as in life. There's my little desk. So, let's make it absolutely tidy. Here's a speck of dust, and there's a spot, I'll have to try and remove them. I try to do it absolutely conscientiously and more or less manage it. So, let's go on. The desk is wobbly, I'll have to steady it, make it firm. I can't, so I try to find something to put under it. I find a scrap of wood and put it under the leg. The desk doesn't wobble any more and it's spick and span. Now I have to set all my things out in perfect order.

I hadn't noticed how totally absorbed I was in what I was doing. I was happy to be doing it – there were my pencils and my penknife, so why not try to make them perfectly sharp? I set about doing it, giving it all my attention, enjoying it, but . . . what's that? There's some hustle and bustle, people start to appear . . . Oh, the rehearsal's beginning. I hear my cue and open the window of my office and start the scene.

We rehearsed *The Embezzlers* every day. Sometimes Stanislavski took the rehearsals, sometimes not. The whole manner of rehearsing, a manner deeply rooted in the Moscow Art Theatre tradition, was quite unusual for me. I was amazed at the new, unexpected methods of working I discovered in the rehearsals Stanislavski took, especially of my own scenes. It was absorbing, fascinating, but, it seemed to me, had nothing to do with the practicalities. Of course, I can achieve certain limited results by doing as he says, but that's not what the audience is going to see. And what's going to happen to the scene I'm about to play? And, strangely, he doesn't seem interested in the actual dialogue. I can't open my mouth without his stopping me, and focusing on some 'little detail' that has nothing to do with anything.

'For heaven's sake, let me get a line out! Something might work.'

'Nothing will work if you're not ready.'

'But I've worked on it.'

'But not on the right thing. What you are doing won't get you into the scene. It's no good your filling your ears with wrong line readings which will be difficult to get rid of later. Don't think of the lines and how to say them, that will happen. Think about what you are doing. So, you, *you*, not some character or other, have to hand out several thousands of roubles to the pay clerks who have gathered at your office. You are responsible down to the very last penny. So, how do you behave? Remember, all these pay clerks are crooks, and you have to be very careful. How are you going to do your job? Where do you begin? Have you got everything ready? What paper, which forms do you need? Have you got enough cash? When you open the window, you estimate how much you need by the number of people you see. Perhaps you can limit the payout to fifty per cent? You have to create a series of practical problems and respond accordingly. Believe me, that is what really matters, that is what the audience will watch, that is what will convince them that the events are real. Can you see how much more there is to this than just words? The way you say the lines comes from what you think, what you do, but you keep leaving out everything that can't be left out in life. When you open your window, you wait for your cue and think how you are going to say your line. But where will that line come from, how can it be living, natural, when you infringe the simplest laws of human behaviour?'

So we started work on being an accountant: counting money, checking forms, drawing up columns, etc., etc. And I started worrying again about the waste of time: we ought to be rehearsing the play. I had a very big role. True, from time to time, this game of accounting was absorbing and I could believe what was happening was meaningful, and if I managed to get a line out here and there it had a warm and truthful ring to it, and produced a good reaction from the other actors. But it was all something of an accident, and so could equally well be lost. And so it proved: as soon as I wanted to pin anything down, and repeat it exactly, it went wrong. The fact is, I didn't feel the kind of security I had been used to in my earlier work: reading the play, rehearsing with the book, setting the moves, looking for the right note for the part, discovering the individual line readings, the 'tricks of the trade', the slow accumulation of the 'treasures' we knew people could easily understand. At that time, the true significance of Stanislavski's work was still a mystery to me. During an intensive, active rehearsal period, nobody appeared to give a thought to the end result – the performance – they seemed to ignore the audience who would come to see them, and, very strange indeed, they paid far greater attention to things the audience wouldn't see.

I won't say that my bewilderment at what I saw at the Moscow Art Theatre created a feeling of disappointment. The opposite: I was absolutely fascinated, it stirred my mind and my imagination, made me want to learn. It was like being back at my first year at theatre school when, full of fear, I made my first acquaintance with the technique and the wonders of the actor's art. All the same, this new method of working seemed rather anarchic.

It was only many years later that the astonishing coherence of Stanislavski's system of working became clear to me – as director, teacher, theatre manager. All these aspects of his practice came together in rehearsal. I came to understand the various phases of his work when developing a performance. I realised that nobody else could feel the shape of the performance as well as he, or take so much care to make it comprehensible to an audience. But he had certain basic approaches which I did not understand.

Work on *The Embezzlers* continued. The play kept changing shape all the time. Work on some scenes had already been transferred to the theatre. The staging was gradually becoming clearer, although none of the actors tried to set their moves and there were frequent moments of improvisation, but that did not concern Stanislavski.

On stage: the old accountant's apartment. His family, consisting of his wife and two children, is worried. Dinnertime has come and gone a while since and he still isn't there. As the tension reaches its peak, there is a sharp ring at the door. The wife runs to the door and opens it and there is her husband and his clerk, Vanechka, totally drunk but in a very convivial mood. They had dropped into an inn, and the accountant, in his cups, had had the idea of marrying his daughter to his bookkeeper. They had then come here, bringing wine and little pasties. But the accountant's wife, a fiery Polish woman, greets them with a stream of bad language the like of which Vanechka, probably, has never heard and he is terrified. The accountant tries to put an end to the mounting quarrel which threatens to turn nasty, and, with some difficulty, takes his wife off into another room so he can explain. Vanechka is left alone, shaken and unhappy. After a while, he starts listening to what the accountant and his wife are doing in their room. He can hear raised voices, but can't make out the words. Vanechka goes right up to the door, the voices drop, he bends down to look through the keyhole and sees the furious woman coming straight towards him and jumps away.

'So what are you going to do?'

'I'm sorry?'

'You're alone in the room . . . in these circumstances you think about what has happened to you, and what you're going to do now. That's your scene.'

'But there's nothing in it! . . . he just stands there, then goes to the door, eavesdrops, looks through the keyhole and jumps away. That's all there is to it.'

'Isn't that enough for you? All right, just go to the door, listen, peep . . . Stop! Are you really listening?'

'Yes.'

'No, you're not. You're trying to do some acting. You're not really hearing anything. Why do you want to eavesdrop?'

'Out of curiosity.'

'I don't think so. All right, just listen. What would you do, if you had to hear and understand what was happening in that room at all costs? You keep wanting to act. Haven't you ever eavesdropped? Try to remember how you did it. All right, let it go. Let's go on. Go and look through the keyhole. A knitting needle is pushed through it straight in your eye. Try to jump away quickly . . . Dreadful. I don't believe any of it, not one movement . . . I don't believe that either . . . What's the problem? Do it again. Why are you so tense?'

We did it over and over, dozens of times. Finally, we got somewhere.

'Good. But there was an extra touch.'

'How do you mean?'

'A little extra touch.'

'I don't understand. What does that mean?'

'It was truthfully done, but you added something to the truth, a scarcely perceptible extra touch, obviously to get a laugh.'

'But shouldn't I do that? After all, it's a funny scene.'

'It will be even funnier if you only do the minimum necessary. That's the most expressive level. Pluses, extras, lead nowhere. They're a big lie. We call that "theatrics". Find the right level — that's the hardest thing in our business. So, try again . . . That's absolutely right. That's what you should always try and do. Understood? Right, let's press on.'

I confess, I still didn't understand very much but I remembered the 'extra touch'. Vanechka is a gentle, modest young man. He turned into an embezzler quite by chance, through a fatal concatenation of circumstances. I have already described his daily concerns, his official activities but there is something else that is, perhaps, the dearest of all to him — his village, Beriozovka, where he spent his childhood, in a broken-down hut, in which his aged mother still lives.

And so we have two 'embezzlers', an old accountant and a bookkeeper, throwing away hundreds and thousands of roubles right, left and centre, travelling from town to town, 'investigating' life's experiences and accidentally, or perhaps not, stumbling on a little town, not far from Vanechka's village. A meeting with some farmers in a tea house has an unsettling, emotional effect on a drunken Vanechka. He tells them that he is a local boy and explains where the village of Beriozovka is, and where the little hut in which his mother lives is to be found.

Vanechka's long speech demands great emotional strength from an actor. A myriad of thoughts and feelings arise in this unhappy young man's head as he recalls what was once dear to him, and is now for ever lost. For me, that speech was the reason everything else in the part existed.

In earlier days I would have started work on the role with this speech. So, let's get to it! But we just don't, we're still caught up in trivia. When will we get to it? Then I'll show how much real feeling, real emotional energy I have. I don't think I'll be accused of 'extra touches'.

I spent many sleepless nights on this speech, looking for all kinds of ways of delivering it, trying my utmost to arouse my feelings. Sometimes it worked, and tears ran down my cheeks as I spoke the words, ' And here . . . is where . . . my mother . . . lives'.

The day for the rehearsal with Stanislavski came. When I started my speech, I was afraid he would stop me and kill my emotion. But, surprisingly, he didn't, and heard me right through to the end. But the expected didn't happen. Feeling vanished and all that was left were some pitiful twitches and a sentimental 'sugary' voice. I was embarrassed and was the first to admit:

'It didn't work.'

'What were you after?'

'At home it worked fine.'

'Meaning?'

'There was a lot of feeling . . . I even cried.'

'And that's what you thought about, "I mustn't lose my feelings"? A wrong task altogether. It ruined things for you. Was that what Vanechka was thinking about when he was speaking to the farmers? Then don't you think about it either. Why should you cry? Let the audience cry.'

'But I think it would be more touching . . .'

'Nonsense. That's cheap sentimentality. That's what untalented hacks do, and they always produce the opposite effect of what they want, they're just annoying. What is Vanechka doing here? What does he want from the farmers? For them to give him his mother's exact address, which is very muddling. And the farmers are quite stupid. Don't you see that this is an active, positive task? Tears have nothing to do with it. Did you imagine all the roads, pathways, landmarks on the way to Beriozovka and your mother's hut? I don't think so, judging by what you just did, yet that is what is important. Imagine the most impenetrable, complicated landscape you can, and try to picture it clearly, watching each of the farmers all the time, to see whether they have understood you, and put any concern for your own experiences and feelings out of your head.'

Suddenly I remembered something. I went on rehearsing. Finally the speech went well and Stanislavski was satisfied. But when I got home, I went back to that sudden memory.

A few years before I joined the Moscow Art Theatre, I was rehearsing a comedy at the Korsh Theatre. The character, the lead role, which I was playing, had fallen on hard times and took a stunt role in a film to earn some money. He had to jump off a cliff into the sea, risking his life. Just before the jump, he turns to the audience, inviting their sympathy, and delivers a long speech, full of dramatic tension, in which he speaks of his miserable life, which has led him to risk death. He doesn't believe he will survive the jump, and so he takes his leave of them for ever and, in his final words, asks the audience to remember him when, after his death, they go to the cinema with their girlfriends and see the scene in which he makes his last appearance on the screen, and plunges into the deep pit of oblivion. They should remember etc., etc.

The speech was very moving, written with great affection, very dramatic, but with a touch of humour, as it should be in a comedy with a happy ending. I liked it very much. I decided not to anticipate the happy ending, but to play the scene straight and dramatically to match the situation. The speech should move the audience deeply so that they are all the more delighted when the happy ending comes.

Working on the speech, that is, reading it through several times, I looked for the key that would release my feelings. Sometimes I was successful, sometimes not. At one rehearsal I was completely successful, my colleagues applauded and congratulated me. I was extremely happy. Overall, the part was a success, all it needed was the finishing touch. Once I'd found it, everything would be fine. The next rehearsal was a disappointment. In the run-up to the speech, I felt great satisfaction at the prospect of even greater success, but it didn't happen. I felt there was something wrong from the very first line, and no matter how hard I tried to put it right, to retrieve what had been so good on the previous day, nothing worked. On the contrary, the more I went on, the worse it got. There was not one living line, not a spark of real-life feeling, it was all dead, empty, artificial. I was so embarrassed I wanted the earth to open up and swallow me. Never mind, I consoled myself, tomorrow I would try to get it together. I would work at home in the evening and everything would be all right. Failure is quite normal.

However, at the next rehearsal and those that followed, things went from bad to worse. Despite all my efforts, the feelings that had come in good rehearsals just would not return. There was only one thing left, the actor's eternal consolation – feeling will come in performance, when there's an audience. The dress rehearsal was a disaster. Finally, after a sleepless night, I went to give the first performance. My first entrance couldn't have been better, everything worked, it was a clear success. Things improved from scene to scene. Not long before the big speech there was a thunderous round of applause. I felt a groundswell of feeling and artistic pleasure. All I had to do was hold on to that until the speech. I tried not to be distracted by anything, I avoided my fellow actors, I stayed alone. Finally, the moment came. I went down to the footlights and said my first line. Someone in the audience, annoyingly, coughed at the end of it. I went on, but for some reason my delivery was very quiet, as though I were afraid of giving vent to what was inside me, but the awful thing was, I could feel there was nothing inside me. The audience started to cough more and more, and I began to get angry with them and with myself. Finally, I decided to 'pull out the stops' a little, which was worse. The audience lost all interest in me and I finished the speech in an incomprehensible gabble. I made an embarrassed exit for my fatal leap, to the total indifference of the audience both to me and to my fate.

A role which was well acted three-quarters of the time had to be judged a total failure, because the moment of climax, up to which everything had led, was bad. Subsequent performances were a repeat of the first. I didn't know what to do to make the feelings I had once experienced return. They refused to come back. They say art is difficult, that you have to work. I knew all that, and I was ready to work to get on top of that damned speech. But how was I to work? What was I to do?

The more I tried, the worse it became. I was overcome with a feeling of shame for my lack of talent – something every actor knows – and in one performance, to ward off this unpleasant feeling, I adopted a tone of cynical indifference to the play and my part in it, particularly as the fatal moment approached. Before the big speech, I chattered with the other actors, told funny stories, laughed, winked at them, and went down to the footlights with complete indifference, looked calmly at the nearest member of the audience and gently tossed the first line straight at him. He sat up and listened. Ah, so you're interested . . . and so are you . . . I look around . . . others are listening to me attentively. Encouraged by this, I went further. The house was quiet. I felt that the whole theatre was interested. I began to worry whether they could hear me in the gallery, whether my thoughts were reaching them. I spoke to them too. I felt that they understood me perfectly and were in sympathy with me. I continued my conversation with them with increasing spirit and enthusiasm, and having ended the speech with an urgent and genuine plea that they should see the film and remember me at the moment when a made my fatal leap, I left the stage to great applause. So that's it! Everything is back to front. You shouldn't concentrate on the role. On the contrary, you should be detached from it in every way you can. That's very easy, very simple. I had discovered a new law! This was not some kind of actor's 'hocus-pocus' which we resort to for the sake of success, and which we can never justify to ourselves. Everything had been convincing and open. How many doors had I knocked at in vain; now, suddenly, here was an unexpected way in.

But at the next performance, my hopes were dashed, my 'discovery' turned out to be illusory. I began to hate the role. Luckily, for me, the play was soon taken off. But it took me a long while to recover from the shock. And now, several years later, rehearsing Vanechka's speech with Stanislavski, I recalled what had happened, and was amazed by the simplicity of the means which this extraordinary master used to open up an actor's creative potential, giving him space for living and genuine feelings to appear. I realised that you genuinely have to concentrate fully on a role if you are to get inside a character. First, you must know where your concentration should be. My failure in the ill-fated play was due to the fact that I had gone off on the wrong track, the opposite way to the one I should have taken, and I had to turn back to get better results. I had accidentally found the path that leads to success. But we are not always so lucky. Rejecting the wrong way doesn't necessarily mean finding the right way to dynamic, genuine action, which Stanislavski demonstrated in our rehearsals on Vanechka's scene. I had come upon that way in the scene I have described when, by chance, I made contact with a member of the audience and received a positive response and then I gradually drew the whole audience into my world and really wanted to make every one of them promise to grant my dying request.

Doesn't Vanechka have the same task when he explains to the peasants where his mother lives? But in the first play I had to make contact not with the people on stage, which is what actors normally have to do, but with the audience, which is rare. That, it seemed to me, was the main reason for what happened with my 'leap'.

The rehearsals I have described with Stanislavski prompted me in that direction. It goes without saying that, at the time, I couldn't have had the relatively clear understanding with which I now write. The shift from the search for inner feelings to the fulfilment of tasks is one of Stanislavski's greatest discoveries, and solves one of the major problems we actors have.

Does that mean he rejected the emotional side of our work? Not at all, he spoke of it every step of the way, and acting only becomes high art when an artist brings genuine emotion and energy to it. But he freed the actor and stopped him torturing himself by his concern with emotion. He stopped him being in love with his own feelings and showed him the right, the natural way to uncover genuine human emotions, that are directed towards fulfilling his tasks, and which actively stimulate other actors.

Many years after the rehearsal I have described, I talked to Stanislavski about the 'creative state', the actor's self-possession and control during performance, and other aspects of *The Embezzlers* rehearsals, and also what had happened at the former Korsh Theatre. I said that concentration and a general seriousness of approach towards a performance did not always give the best results. Many actors are convinced that a touch of light-hearted-ness, of indifference and cynicism towards their work, often brings them much greater success. Every actor knows times when, for some reason, he wants to play particularly well and he ends up playing much worse. That happens when 'someone or other' is seeing the show. The actor marshals his forces, concentrates, but in most cases he is a total failure.

I very carefully indicated to Stanislavski that sometimes I, too, was of that opinion as, more than once, it had been confirmed by my own experience, especially when I was giving a reading. As a reader I only had rare success, and that was on those evenings when I was in a hurry to go somewhere after the recital, say to meet someone.

'And why do you think you read well?'

'From the way I felt, and . . .'

'And . . .'

'Because the audience liked it . . .'

'Both may have been delusions.'

'But the managers and the people there, after my reading, said that . . .'

'Hm! These potboilers. When you played badly, it wasn't because you had concentration and control, and a serious attitude, and all the other essentials an artist needs. The simple fact is you didn't concentrate properly, and that is where the trouble lies. The wrong kind of concentration is a stumbling block, and once you have removed it, you are better. If you can concentrate your genuine human powers of attention on fulfilling a concrete task in performance, you will be really good.'

Neither my theatre school nor the directors I worked with subsequently provided me with an understanding of rhythm. In the years immediately preceding my entry into the Moscow Art Theatre I often heard this word on the lips of some professionals, but they didn't give me a very clear understanding of its nature (I'm talking about rhythm in relation to theatre), so, for me, this extremely important question was still unresolved.

Until now, I had also never been given a clear definition of rhythm. It is a matter of shame to acknowledge that rhythm, tempo, tempo-rhythm, rhythm-tempo fall frequently from the lips of directors, actors, theatre scholars and critics. But try to get a precise definition of what these words mean from any of them and they will answer in vague generalisations which are of no practical value and won't satisfy your curiosity in the slightest. In earlier periods, in theatre jargon, there was the almost universal word 'tone'. There was a tone for the role, a 'general tone' for the play, and an actor either found the 'tone' or he didn't. There could be a performance when the tone was 'under' and, in mid-action, an actor just before his entrance would be asked to 'lift' it, although no one knew how that was to be done, and so, when he went on, the actor just started talking louder than the rest. That was no good, the actor didn't 'find the tone' and soon lost heart, so the action continued to be 'under' until something happened, despite the cast, and the tone 'lifted' and that was a pretext for a quarrel among the actors. It was always inconclusive because no one really knew what had happened and what the 'tone of the performance', with which they were so concerned, meant.

I think what they were looking for was the idea that Stanislavski later defined as rhythm. I had the opportunity to see how he applied his knowledge of the subject in rehearsal. I saw how a slow, plodding scene was magically transformed into a full-blooded, action-packed event in which the conflict was intense because of the masterly way he put his very precise ideas on dramatic rhythm into practice. For example, we were rehearsing a little scene from *The Embezzlers*. The old accountant, who is travelling with his bookkeeper on a goods train, falls into the clutches of card sharps, starts to play and risks losing all of the embezzled money that is still in Vanechka's wallet. This horrifies the poor bookkeeper. They arrive at a station and the accountant ends the game and goes to the buffet for some vodka. The train is stopping for a while. Vanechka leaps off the train, goes to his partner in the hope of persuading him not to go back to the compartment, rather to stay where he is, or, at least, to distract his attention so that he doesn't notice the train is leaving. But the overexcited accountant is not so easily tricked. He is obsessed by the idea of winning back the money he has lost, and it is very difficult to keep him in the buffet when the bell rings to announce the imminent departure of the train, the more so since Vanechka has no lines apart from exclaiming: 'Fillip Stepanovich! Fillip Stepanovich!' That's all the writer gives him. The scene didn't work and I felt it was all my fault but turned the blame back on the writer. After all, what can you do when all you have is one line!

It was all right for Tarkhanov, who played the scene superbly. He had lots of words, something to act with, whereas all I had was one sentence, 'Fillip Stepanovich! Fillip Stepanovich!', and that was all.

So imagine my surprise when Stanislavski said:

'Remember, this is your scene, you have the lead role, not Tarkhanov.'

'But all I have is "Fillip Stepanovich!" '

'That's not the point. You have a highly active task. You hold on to the accountant at any price, and stop him boarding the train. The way you do that will demonstrate your skill.'

'But I haven't any words to do it with, it's very hard . . .'

'The words aren't what matters. Try to keep an eye simultaneously on Tarkhanov and on the stationary train, which is about to leave. That is your salvation. Try it.'

'Try it!' Easier said than done. How? I just stood there in confusion.

'Right, where is Tarkhanov and where is the train? Try to establish everything quite precisely. Look at Tarkhanov. What he is doing and what the train is doing. Can you feel the rhythm of this scene?'

There! The word 'rhythm'. I haven't the slightest notion what it means.

Then he continues:

'You're not standing in the right rhythm! . . .

Standing in rhythm! How do you stand in rhythm? Walk, dance, sing, yes, but stand?

'Would you stand like that if you were seriously threatened by Tarkhanov's getting on the train?'

'I'm sorry, but I don't understand the meaning of rhythm.'

'That doesn't matter. In the corner, there's a mouse. Take a stick, lie in wait for it and kill it as soon as it jumps out. No, that way you will miss. Watch it closely, closely. As soon as I clap my hands, hit it. Now, you see, you were too late. Try again . . . and again. Concentrate and try to make the blow coincide with the clap. Now, you see, you're standing in a different rhythm from before. Can you feel the difference? Standing and watching the mouse is one rhythm, watching a tiger creep up on you is another. Watch Tarkhanov carefully, observe all his actions. He has forgotten about the train, his mind is on refreshment. For you, that's good. You can relax for a moment and look at what the train is doing. You can even run out on to the platform for a moment, come back quickly and concentrate on Tarkhanov. Try to guess his intentions and read his thoughts. He's remembered the train and is rummaging in his pockets so he can pay for the vodka. Get yourself ready to keep him in the buffet at any cost. Your readiness to complete an action will force you into a different rhythm from the one you are in now. So, try it.'

I was deeply involved in this aspect of acting technique, the rhythm. I continued to rehearse with enthusiasm, tried to grasp its essence, but couldn't. I couldn't do any of the things Stanislavski suggested. Sometimes I was very fast and busy, but lost all sight of my fellow actor; sometimes, on the other hand, I managed to pay him some attention, but then all my movements were slow and heavy.

Stanislavski tried many different ways to set me on the right path and demonstrated brilliantly his own capacity to master various rhythms. He would take some very simple event from life, for example buying a newspaper at a station kiosk, and play it in different rhythms. He would buy it when he had an hour to wait and didn't know how to kill the time, or when the first or second bell had sounded, or when the train was already moving. The actions were the same but in completely different rhythms. He could do this exercise in any order, speeding up or slowing down, whichever. It was amazing. I realised that he has achieved this control through continuous work. I saw the mastery, the technique, the real, visible technique of acting.

Of all the things I had seen and understood in my earlier rehearsals with Stanislavski, that was what excited me most. I still couldn't really do anything, but I understood that this was very important for an actor, and I felt that, in the end, it could be mastered, and I realised it was something akin to exercises for the violin, or technical music exercises – études – in general. I knew that, as a former musician. The same étude can be played in different rhythms, with different bowing, to meet different ends. I knew what a pleasure it was when the fingers are free and they acquire confidence, flexibility and dexterity, so that the musician never has any doubts that an exercise, conscientiously and regularly practised for a period of time, will develop his technique. In these rehearsals, when Stanislavski gave such a dazzling display of the ease and simplicity of his rhythm technique, I clearly saw an affinity with the other arts.

'What are you thinking about? It's really very simple. Try to live in another rhythm. You can use externals to find it. Sit down quickly, stand up, sit down again, change your position ten, twelve times a second without thinking about it. Conduct this scene, musically. How would you conduct it if you were asked? . . . No, not *andante*, this is *presto*. Remember, keeping Tarkhanov in the buffet, or not, is a matter of life and death. If this were really the case, would you take much time to think? What would you do?'

We hadn't noticed how engrossed we had become in our game. Tarkhanov tried to leave the room, but, without touching him physically, I didn't let him. That was an absolute condition, and the game quickly turned into a serious contest. We found more subtle ways of continuing the struggle. Stanislavski understood the situation, said nothing and held back. That was what he wanted. The game became more and more heated. Suddenly the bell rang for the train. We relaxed.

'Why have you stopped?'

'It's over, the train's gone – it's no good quarrelling any more.'

'Nothing of the sort, it's only just begun! That was only the second bell. There's a third and then a whistle. You only calm down after the whistle, then battle is over. In the meantime, it goes on, the rhythm gets faster and faster . . . Go on.'

We renewed our struggle and Stanislavski ordered that the third bell and the whistle should only sound on his cue. He kept us in this intense quarrel for about twenty minutes more, but we didn't feel our invention flagging. On the contrary, we were carried away, we developed greater depth, greater variety, greater intensity, and when, finally, the bell rang, announcing the departure of the train and the end of the conflict between the accountant and book-keeper, I felt rather sorry that our enthralling game had come to an end. It was so good to feel that beating pulse, that dynamism inside me! I was happy I had found different ways to communicate with Tarkhanov. I was surprised that you could create a scene like that out of nothing. All that I had in my script was the same thing over and over again, 'Fillip Stepanovich! Fillip Stepanovich!' Any actor in my place would have said like me: 'There's nothing to act here.' So, who would have thought it?

It was only a minor scene, and so, later, it was heavily cut. This incident couldn't actually be performed in the way I have described it. But the work we had done had a beneficial effect. Although brief, this scene was quite convincing. In those rehearsals, for the first time, I experienced, albeit vaguely, an understanding of theatrical rhythm, which, later, was developed, refined and found an even more important place in my professional work. It became a miraculous means for solving theatrical problems.

*

Rehearsals continued and every session produced a fresh discovery. Even in rehearsal you could feel the play taking shape. Soon the run-throughs began. Stanislavski's work took on a quite different character. True, from time to time he would stop over an entrance. I remember that happened when we were rehearsing the scene in the railway compartment where the accountant and the bookkeeper mistake the travelling salesman of some lithograph business for a police detective. Stanislavski suddenly concentrated on the salesman's entrance into the carriage. With rare persistence he tried to achieve some goal that we could not understand, niggling over every detail, every movement. This wearisome work went on for two or three hours. We all began to lose patience, especially the actor playing the salesman, and we all wondered what would happen later, when we came to play the whole scene, which wasn't going very well. But Stanislavski wanted to get something from the salesman, so it looked as though he had lost interest in what was coming next. We understood what he wanted. He wanted the salesman to come in as though he were a real professional detective, on the trail of some crooks, determined not to let a golden opportunity for fame slip. The effect was remarkable and both Tarkhanov and I were terrified. We played the scene with great truth. Stanislavski didn't stop but only suggested to Tarkhanov: 'When the tension is at its height, you try and light a cigarette, but you drop it, so it misses the match.'

Tarkhanov did so with wonderful skill. The people at the rehearsal burst out laughing.

Then Stanislavski turned his attention to the props. There were children's toys that the accountant had won somewhere. They were rather crude. Stanislavski looked at them and, turning to Tarkharnov, said:

'We need proper toys. These are too crude to match the subtlety of your acting.'

He went on to the next scene.

Let me just say, however, that spending time over individual scenes like this was now the exception rather than the rule. He was presently concerned with a broader problem: to bring together all the work done in rehearsal and shape it into a play.

Finally, the play opened. Tarkhanov and Batalov played splendidly, and there were good moments in the production. But the weakness of the material, dramatically speaking, and the absence of any exciting ideas undermined the quality of the performance. And without ideas Stanislavski could not create a work of art. For all his mastery, he could not draw anything out of this slack, superficial play. The audience saw that it was a series of skilfully directed, excellently played incidents, without any definite idea where it was going or its immediate relevance. That gave a master like Stanislavski no satisfaction. Work on the play caused him, as an artist, anxiety and pain. The play soon came off. In a letter Stanislavski sent me on the occasion of the twenty-fifth anniversary of my debut in the theatre, he wrote, 'I remember our hard but joyous work on *Dead Souls* and the hard but joyless work on *The Embezzlers*.'

I was not sure whether my acting was any good or not. It was the first part I played at the Moscow Art Theatre and success or failure was extremely important. I got mixed reviews – good, bad and indifferent. 'Here,' some said, 'is a fine actor who went back to school and died.' As I said, I was not sure whether I was any good or not. But however that may be, the play went on, and initially was done quite often. My performance was soon 'run in' and even had some outstanding moments that were well received and sometimes even applauded. Not in the first performances. I was pleased. 'This,' I thought, 'is the fruit of Stanislavski's work. What a pity he can't see the show! No matter, somehow he will.' And, in fact, he soon did.

In the spring, Stanislavski took us on tour to Leningrad. *The Embezzlers* was in the repertoire. Leningrad had a special meaning for me. This was my home. My best memories are there – my theatre school, the Aleksandrinski and the Suvorin theatres, where my artistic career began.

In Leningrad many of my friends and acquaintances were at the rehearsals of *The Embezzlers*. They were either extras or had come to see how meticulously Stanislavski worked on a revival, particularly when the Moscow Art Theatre was on tour. But I felt calm. My performance was now very polished and all I wanted was to show the brilliance of my acting to Stanislavski and the people I knew who were at rehearsals.

The rehearsal began with the scene in the inn, a difficult crowd scene. I was not in the first part. I came on later. All went smoothly up to my entrance. Then it was me. I waited impatiently for my cue and then ran on stage. I was very pleased with the way I ran in, today particularly, and suddenly:

'Stop!'

The rehearsal halted and everybody froze. I didn't understand why we had stopped. Anyway, it wasn't my fault. I was on good form today.

'Awful! What are you doing? Who told you to do that?' then, after some whispering with his assistants, 'I mean you, Toporkov!'

I was genuinely amazed. 'What is it?'

'That, dear boy, is the way they act in Kharkov. Awful!'

I took a side look at my Leningrad friends who were gazing at me with curiosity and pity from the stalls.

'Once again, please, be so kind.'

I ran in again and again came 'Stop'.

'You ran in to do some "acting", you already knew what, where and how things would happen. Why do you run into the inn? To convey important news to Fillip Stepanovich. Do you know where he is sitting? Well then, what are you going to do? And what about rhythm? Rhythm! Why this ponderous rhythm. Again. Oh, dear, dear, dear!'

And the whole four-hour rehearsal was spent on my running in. When he got what he wanted, Stanislavski ended the rehearsal, having done only one scene.

The next day was the second and final rehearsal of *The Embezzlers*. Stanislavski didn't have very much time to spend on individual parts of the play but I could feel how closely he was watching me throughout, and during the evening performance. After the show, I was told that Stanislavski would like to see me at his hotel the following day for a chat.

He greeted me courteously and warmly in his room and began, a little embarrassed, 'Well, dear boy, you've forgotten everything I taught you. What you are doing is awful, you're going back to the old ways.'

'I was a bit off in yesterday's rehearsal and that's why my performance in the evening didn't work, but up till now, at the Art Theatre I've been quite successful and audiences have taken to me.'

'It's very sad that you think about acting in that way. Audiences sometimes like the wrong thing. I had an anonymous telephone call. The caller was horrified by your performance.'

I didn't know then that the 'anonymous' caller was a bogeyman Stanislavski used as a way of getting to an actor. He invented this 'anonymous' person as someone impartial, as opposed to himself, who was rather too inclined to find fault.

In the course of a long conversation he explained to me what the role had once been and what it had become.

'Once you found an unbroken, organic line of action in the role, and went from event to event in pursuit of your goal. Later, in performance, by their reactions, the audience showed you the successful bits, and you started to concentrate on them, held on to them, and started to spotlight them. You were so in love with them, with the way you said the lines, and did the moves, you ignored everything else. You were impatient for those favourite moments when you won cheap laurels, and the role suffered, it fell apart, it lost its sense as a whole, its purpose. Earlier you had the impression your performance was pallid. That may well be, but you acted truthfully, and you should have built on the truth you had discovered, strengthened the through-action, not run after individual effects. That would have led to a really radiant performance. But you went in quite another direction. Remember what I told you, be wary of taking the wrong track, of acting individual little bits, playing for cheap applause during a scene, or on your exit. Look at the part as a whole. Let the audience follow the logic of your struggle, get them interested in what happens to you, so that they can't take their eyes off you, so that they're not only afraid to applaud, but even to make the slightest move that would prevent them from seeing all the subtleties of your behaviour. That is real acting. It doesn't entertain, it strikes deep into the heart of an audience.'

In the gap between two crucial productions I did with Stanislavski, I met him from time to time, either just for a chat, or sometimes to watch him working on productions in which I did not appear. On one occasion I learned that Stanislavski was going to revive *The Cherry Orchard* and he asked me to attend rehearsals as I was going to understudy Moskvin in the role of Epikhodov.[1] The news would have excited me considerably at any time, but especially then, and for this reason.

Some twenty years before the events I am describing, the Moscow Art Theatre had been on tour in Petersburg and I saw them perform for the first time. It was *The Cherry Orchard*. I have already described the impression it made on me. After the show I

[1] Ivan Moskvin, one of the founder members of the Moscow Art Theatre had created the role in 1904. Rehearsals began in May 1928.

went to the theatre club on Litieni Prospekt, a place where actors liked to gather. But that evening I wasn't drawn to the usual attractions – the gaming tables, the bar. I wanted to be alone and think over what I had seen at the theatre. I was sitting in a chair in one of the comfortable rooms at the club when one of the public's favourite actors, Yuriev – a wonderful artist and man of rare qualities – came in. Although somewhat reserved on the outside he was generally gentle and kind to people and he was very warm towards me in particular. I was told he had a very flattering opinion of my graduation performances at the Aleksandrinski Theatre, and now his exceptional pleasant, velvety voice drew me out of my reverie:

'A penny for your thoughts.'

He sat down beside me and we began to talk. The dimly lit room, the comfortable armchair and everything else kept us talking until dawn. We started with the Moscow Art Theatre. Yuriev shared much of my enthusiasm for its art, but he criticised it also, sometimes quite severely, defending his beloved Aleksandrinski Theatre and the Maly in Moscow. We talked about theatre, acting and our creative problems. Yuriev was one of the actors who constantly, doggedly, worked on themselves, perfecting their technique. For them, the only way of reaching the heights, or somewhere near it, was through work. As we parted at first light, I once again poured out my enthusiasm for *The Cherry Orchard* and especially for Moskvin who was wonderful as Epikhodov. And I moaned a little about my own prospects. Saying goodbye, he took my hand and said: 'My dear friend, you have no need to worry about your future. Your gifts are not in doubt. Start to work the way you should, you will soon be noticed, you'll be able to choose the theatre you like, and after twenty years, you know, you'll come back here on tour with the Art Theatre and you will be playing Epikhodov, and I will applaud you.'

At the time, I though he was just showing his usual kindness, but his words gave me a warm glow.

I remembered this occasion when I was asked to understudy Moskvin, and I especially recalled it when I really did go to Leningrad and played Epikhodov. It was twenty years after my conversation with Yuriev at the theatre club on Litieni Prospekt.

When he was reviving *The Cherry Orchard*, Stanislavski tried, as always, to eliminate clichés from the actors' performances. But this time he did not limit himself merely to doing that, but, it seemed to me, tried to revise his original interpretation of the play, removing all remaining traces of sentimentality, trying to take a more contemporary view of the events. He only succeeded in part. Limited rehearsal and some resistance from the cast prevented him from fully achieving his goal.[1]

Moskvin rehearsed Epikhodov and I was just a 'reserve', taking the opportunity when he was absent to try out some scenes, but Stanislavski wasn't present. He had no time to work with me, particularly as he was playing Gaev. Only fleetingly, when his eye fell on me, did he give me one or two ideas to think about.

'Remember, if you try to play an idiot, you'll get nowhere. He is a passionate Spaniard and very "civilised", but his face . . .' He pushed up the tip of his nose with his finger, making is face look unbelievably ridiculous. 'And don't be tricksy, play him straight, civilised, someone who, it is true, can't go anywhere without bumping into something or knocking something over, or creating havoc. But he regards all these things as his fate. It's useless to fight. You can only smile.'

The first time I played Epikhodov, Stanislavski inspected my make-up before the show, gave me a lot of last-minute advice and kept an eye on me, whenever possible, throughout the performance. In the first act there was a remarkable piece of directing. Everyone has gone to meet Ranievskaya. The stage is empty. In the distance the jingling bells of an approaching carriage can be heard, then distant voices then the meeting of the new arrivals with the people waiting for them, cries of joy, laughter, kisses, etc. At first you can hardly hear all this, then it all becomes louder and louder, it comes nearer and nearer until it is right upon you and Ranievskaya excitedly runs on to the stage with all the rest following her . . . After that, everything is as in the script. All this off-stage action was the result of the director's imagination and long, hard work, and had a wonderful effect on the audience. Technically this was achieved by having the actors way backstage, on a stairway behind an iron door. As the scene progresses, the iron door is opened slightly, then wider until it is completely open. The actors come through it and run towards the stage in a crowd, acting Ranievskaya's arrival, and the play continues.

---

[1] The lack of rehearsal time was due to the last-minute decision by the authorities not to allow a planned production of *Uncle Vanya*. They suggested *The Cherry Orchard* instead.

The first time I played Epikhodov, I was somewhat flustered and when I got to the iron door on the stairs it was already shut and all the other actors were on the other side. I was afraid to open it and stayed where I was and waited for them to open it, so I could join them in the scene. When I came on with the others, Stanislavski gave me a sideways look and I understood that he'd had a sudden thought about me. At the end of the act he called me to his dressing-room and asked: 'Why weren't you in your proper place?'

'I'm sorry, I was confused and got lost backstage.'

'But when you found yourself on the wrong side of the door, did you take part in the scene?'

'Yes, yes, of course,' I lied.

'Dreadful! . . . You ruined the scene. Oh dear, oh dear! In the first place, how could you play the scene when you couldn't see us? Then there's a difference in sound. When we are behind the door our voices are muffled, but once beyond it your voice sounds quite different. That's not right. The scene is very subtle, it is all nuances, and you ruined them.'

I stood there in embarrassment.

'On the whole, your performance is quite good. But why do you trip in the doorway on your first exit? To show us from the start you are a comic character? Why the visiting card? The role must develop gradually. It is much better if the audience takes you seriously at first. That's to your advantage. By developing the role and showing the audience new aspects of your character all the time, you will be able to hold their interest throughout. So why tell them, "Remember, I'm a comedy part, I'm going to make you laugh," at the outset? The audience will make up its own mind who you are. Your job is to follow the through-action absolutely straight, then you will be playing high, not low, comedy.'

Much later, when I was more secure in *The Cherry Orchard*, and had played Epikhodov several times, Stanislavski called a rehearsal in his apartment in Leontievski Lane. One of the young actors was being rehearsed in as Dunyasha, or Yasha or Charlotta, I can't remember which. They showed Stanislavski the beginning of Act Two where Epikhodov, Yasha, Dunyasha and Charlotta are sitting in a field and talking. We played the whole scene through. Stanislavski was silent for a long time, then said: 'I don't think you fully understand what a work of genius this scene is. Do you realise the kind of people Chekhov has assembled here? Such a combination, if you think about it, can't help being funny. There's a wealth of humour in it. Think about it. There's a stupid, fat, healthy country girl [Dunyasha] who imagines she is a sickly, delicate, refined young lady. Next to her there are two jealous lovers. One is a clumsy, pigeon-toed ignoramus, convinced of his sophistication and learning, and of being "fated". The other is a young country bumpkin, who has spent a few years in Paris and so imagines himself to be at the very least a French aristocrat, a marquis. And, added to the group, there's a German governess, who was once a horseback rider in a circus and a fairground actress, an eccentric who speaks poor Russian. They are all trying to impress each other. One with the subtlety of his feelings and experiences, another with her refined manners, a third with his sophistication and knowledge, a fourth with her extremely colourful life story. Nobody wants to listen to anybody else, they are only thinking about themselves. You see what an active task that is: to get everyone's attention, to belittle other people's merits, force them to listen to you, and then there is the tangled love plot with Yasha, Dunyasha and Epikhodov. That is real humour, that is Chekhov's genius. How are you going to approach it? How are you going to play it? Here we have the truth of life, here we have Chekhov's genuine subtlety, a total absence of exaggeration and yet, at the same time, broad humour. Every actor must follow his own line in this scene and play it straight, convinced of his own importance. The more seriously the battle between the two rivals is conducted, with both very subtle diplomacy and direct threats with a revolver (what Spanish passion), the closer you will get to Chekhov. Don't waste your time on tiny tricks, don't turn high art into cheap farce, banality. Be strict with yourselves as artists. Chekhov was and that's why he was able to reach the heights of humour.'

Subsequent meetings with Stanislavski prior to starting work on *Dead Souls* have left little trace in my memory. Evidently they were not frequent and of no great significance. But from the moment work began on the play until the end, every rehearsal, every discussion with him is firmly fixed in my mind, and so tiny details suddenly return with such vividness they could have happened yesterday.

Working on the role of Chichikov was a very important moment in my career. Now I was able consciously to understand things in the Stanislavski system which had been vague before. That didn't happen overnight. I followed a difficult path. There was a great deal of pain, many shocks, failures, frustrations, but nothing could shake my belief that I was on the right path, the one Stanislavski had shown me. And although this path did not lead me to success in the early performances, it did finally set me on the way I had dreamed of since school. I had wandered in darkness looking for it. For me this was an opportunity in my career to move forward.

The reader who is familiar with the working process I have described will realise it is difficult for me to give a theoretical explanation. So, I will pass on to an explanation of something which seems to me of greater interest, the memory of my encounters with Stanislavski as we worked on *Dead Souls*.

Dead Souls

On 15 September 1932, Sakhnovski,[1] the director of *Dead Souls*, wrote in the magazine, *Soviet Art*: 'The work which Stanislavski did with the cast of *Dead Souls* represents one of the most significant chapters in the history of the Art Theatre. Some rehearsals were fully recorded verbatim, others partially. They will remain in the memory of all who were present, not only as a remarkable demonstration of directing by a man of genius, but also of new methods in creating a role. At some rehearsals, the cast applauded Stanislavski wildly as he revolutionised the way of representing familiar things.'

The very particular circumstances surrounding this production obliged Stanislavski to work miracles. He mobilised all his skills, all his genius as a director and a teacher, and those who were present at rehearsals could not but be dazzled by his mastery and talent. What were these special circumstances that gave Stanislavski's energy such a boost? I will try and explain briefly.

In those not too far distant times, many of our theatres were in the grip of hardline formalism.[2] In the search for 'greater expressiveness' and 'progressive trends', they got lost among the tiny byways of a vulgar kind of pseudo-sociology, using 'heightened' form and external exaggeration, which at the time went by the fashionable name of the Grotesque. It was like a directors' orgy. There was much genuine enthusiasm on the part of talented directors, particularly the young ones, a great deal of naive imitation by mediocrities and amateurs, and there were clever adventurers who loved to fish in troubled waters.

There is a very interesting book to be written about the

[1] After his return from America in 1924, Stanislavski worked with his assistants, who knew his methods and took preliminary rehearsals. He would then rework what they had done. After his illness much of the work was done in his apartment.

[2] Formalism, represented notably by Meyerhold and Eisenstein, had been condemned in 1934 on Stalin's orders. Socialist Realism became the order of the day. Writing in the late 1940s, Toporkov is toeing the party line. This whole section needs to be read within that political context.

nonsensical aberrations of these 'innovators'. The well-structured, monumental works that make up our dramatic literature were cut up into tiny episodes and then a 'work' was cobbled together that looked more like a patchwork quilt. At the director's whim, the characters were distorted out of all recognition, they were nowhere near the author's original intentions. For instance, in one of Ostrovski's plays, *The League of Nations*, the characters were often on a trapeze or walked a tightrope.

The arty critics were, of course, on the side of the 'innovators'. They were extremely active and aggressive and literally fell upon on anything in the theatre that showed any degree of sane thinking. Of course, their shafts were mostly directed against the Moscow Art Theatre, which tried not only to preserve its realist tradition, but to develop it in the direction of socialist realism, to which the production of a play like Ivanov's *The Armoured Train 14–69* bears witness.[1]

However, Sakhnovski began rehearsals with more than a nod in the direction of the Grotesque. I don't know whether Stanislavski or Nemirovich-Danchenko took any part in the preparatory work, but, at all events, they weren't present at rehearsals.

Sakhnovksi was a director with a very individual frame of mind, and was only just beginning to find his way at the Moscow Art Theatre. His search for heightened means of expression was irrepressible but not yet sufficiently tempered by a knowledge of the way we directed plays. He was a highly educated man, he thought and spoke in grandiose, glittering paradoxes, and his work with actors had a somewhat paradoxical character. He did not work practically, like a professional director, his work was more literary and philosophical. We did all sorts of things to try and get deeper into Gogol's play but, unfortunately, they were irrelevant to our needs.

We had endless discussions with him. There was a great deal of witty speculation about Gogol's personality, his view of the world and his relationship to his contemporaries, etc., etc. We went to museums to look at various portraits, studied his works, his letters and his biography. To deepen our awareness that we were dealing with the dead, he suggested to me that I visit a cemetery. What he had to say was always of interest and engaging, but it was too

---

[1] Opened 8 November 1927. The production was regarded as one of the finest examples of new Soviet theatre.

vague. However many times we went to the cemetery, museums, art galleries, however many times we engaged in fascinating discussions, it was all too abstract and too much dead weight as far as practical work was concerned. We all applied ourselves with great enthusiasm, discovering things, losing others but, in general, we floundered, having no precise sense of where we were going, until the dress rehearsal when Stanislavski arrived. I won't describe the dress rehearsal in detail and my impressions of it. I will only say that after it Stanislavski was completely at a loss. He told the directors that he understood nothing of what he had seen, that we had gone down a blind alley and that we would have to throw everything out and start all over again. Something of the sort.

I wasn't present at the discussions Stanislavski had with the directors and Bulgakov, who had done the adaptation, and with his other collaborators, so I can only report roughly what was said from what I was told by the people I have mentioned, and also from what Stanislavski personally told me later.

Recalling all the tiny details of the work Stanislavski did on *Dead Souls*, all the things he taught us during rehearsals, I think I am able to indicate, quite accurately, the path he took to save the play.

His first task, undoubtedly, was to find the dramatic centre of a flawed script. How was he to build the storyline? What should the audience see? Not one of the adaptations of Gogol's novel had ever been successful on stage (there had been more than a hundred of them). The reason was its dramatic looseness. In earlier times individual scenes from *Dead Souls* had been played with great success. But put them all together into a single evening, and you merely have a series of scenes repeatedly dealing with the purchase of dead souls, without any central thematic development, and that cannot hold the audience's attention sufficiently on the course of events. They start to get bored halfway through even when there are outstanding actors like Varlamov, Davydov, and Dalmatov.

The most thankless role in all those adaptations was Chichikov, a creation of genius. He goes right through the play, but as he repeats the same thing over and over in every scene, the audience soon gets tired of him, and they pay him little or no attention, the more so since he is surrounded by merchants, farmers and officials – a gallery of typical Gogol characters.

But it was on Chichikov that Stanislavski decided to base the thematic development of the play. The adaptation was slightly altered and that was the version that Stanislavski accordingly rehearsed.

'Chichikov's Progress' – that was to be the subject of the play, that's what the audience was supposed to see, Stanislavski decided. Does that mean he limited the production to that single task? Naturally not. He respected the theatre and its laws, and he knew that the better a play is constructed, the better it is able to convey ideas. If a play is flawed, it is the director's job to improve it, not by adding irrelevant flourishes which distract the audience from the essentials, but by making the through-action stronger.

At one rehearsal Stanislavski said:

'What are we going to do about Chichikov? How are we going to get around the fact that he keeps turning up and has the same conversation with monotonous regularity? The only answer is the through-action. We have to be able to show how a chance event suggests a plan to buy dead souls, how this plan beings to grow, matures, reaches its climax and then totally collapses. If you master the through-action in this role, I'll raise my hat to you. But it's going to be difficult.'

The task Stanislavski had set was difficult both in general and in particular. Having chosen Chichikov as the hero of the play, he did not have an actor who was up to the role. My theatrical talents may have been adequate for the consciously 'grotesque' figure we had unfortunately tried to create until Stanislavski started work, but it was not at all adequate for the genuine Chichikov of Gogol's novel. Moreover, our attempts to distort Gogol's character, to create a grotesque, a mask instead of a living person, to 'heighten' a character that was perfectly heightened already, had, naturally, distorted any idea of truth we had, of what seemed probable, human or natural, and paralysed my instinct and will to create.

Prevailing theatrical fashion had led us to take a wrong approach at the very start of rehearsal, and had led us up a blind alley, and only someone of considerable practical learning could get us out.

'You are completely out of joint,' Stanislavski told me in our first discussion after the dress rehearsal. 'Not one part of you is whole. We need to treat you, to reset all your bones. You have to learn to walk again, not act, just walk.'

These, briefly, are the basic circumstances which Stanislavski had to overcome, so that from the very beginning we could tell in theatrical form the simple story of the progress of the minor official Chichikov properly. Stanislavski never spoke to us of the major tasks this play presented him with before the time was right. That was his system.

'Can you bargain?' he asked me.

'Bargain?'

'Yes, buy cheap, sell dear, throw dust in the buyer's eyes, advance your own interests and block other people's, guess his prices, say you're poor, swear your life away, etc.?'

'No, not at all.'

'You'll have to learn. It's the most important thing for your role.'

In the first rehearsals, Stanislavski called just me, so as to treat my dislocated limbs. He worked carefully with me and with great attention, like a doctor with a patient and, as I now understand, we were concerned with the creation and shaping of the organic line of Chichikov's physical behaviour. That was his method of treatment, a method which he subsequently advanced as the best for achieving the ultimate goal of creating a fully rounded character, a method which later came to be called the 'Method of Physical Action'.

Work began with discussions, but they were nothing like the discussions we had had previously. Stanislavski brought us right back down to earth. The questions he asked astonished us by their simplicity, clarity and practicality. I was even a little disappointed and puzzled. It was all too simple, mundane and far removed from those goals we had dimly perceived. Moreover, the earlier work we had done had so dulled my wits that I had the greatest difficulty answering the simplest question.

'So, why does Chichikov buy dead souls?' Stanislavski suddenly asked me.

What could I answer? Everybody knew why, but . . .

'Why? It says so in the book. He mortgages them to the board of guardians and so gets money.'

'Why?'

'Why?'

'What's the advantage, why does he need money, what will he do with it? Have you thought about that?'

'Not in that detail.'

'Then do it.'

(Long pause.)

'So, the souls have been mortgaged, you've got the money, now what?

(Another pause.)

'You need to know down to the last detail what is the specific purpose of everything you do. Think it through thoroughly, run through Chichikov's life story, and gather material you can work on.'

Stanislavski gently, artfully led me to the ideas he wanted, but never gave ready-made answers. He just succeeded in arousing my imagination.

'Put yourself in Chichikov's place. What would you do in these circumstances?'

'But I'm not Chichikov, I'm not interested in profit.'

'But if you were, what if you were enormously interested, what would you do?'

In these discussions we determined the simplest, most mundane things about Chichikov's life. There was nothing obscure or abstruse about them, nothing that the representatives of militant formalism of the period were so fond of, as Andrei Bely wrote in his sharply critical article 'Unknown Gogol' aimed at the Art Theatre: 'Just a few words more about symbolic detail in Gogol's text. *Dead Souls* opens with a description of Chichikov's coach. The peasants who happened to be present at his arrival commented on the wheels of his coach. Among the souls mortgaged to Chichikov by Korobochka, who played such a fateful role in his unmasking, was a peasant called Koleso [wheel]. At the moment when Chichikov fled from the provincial capital, it was discovered that the wheel of the carriage was damaged.'

I only introduce this extract to state that in his work on *Dead Souls*, Stanislavski was not interested in such 'symbolic details'. He considered this kind of analysis was irrelevant 'hogwash'. Initially, what interested him were Chichikov's simplest, living, real concerns: how much money he had, when he gave the Secretary to the Board of Guardians a bribe, and how big it was, etc.

He demanded a knowledge of the character's life in the minutest detail. I had to answer all these questions for myself. I answered them while waiting to begin work proper. Work had, in fact, already begun but the method was unusual for me.

Prologue

We hardly noticed the moment when we passed from discussion to action. We forgot about games and started rehearsing the Prologue. Here is the script of the Prologue in the adaptation of *Dead Souls*.

PROLOGUE

A room in an inn in the capital.

CHICHIKOV: Mr Secretary!

SECRETARY: Mr Chichikov! You again? What does this mean? In the morning you pester me in the Board of Guardians office, and in the evening you seize upon me at the inn. Let me alone. I have already explained, my dear man, that I can do nothing for you.

CHICHIKOV: As you wish, Excellency, but I am not leaving here until I get an answer.

SECRETARY: Your employer is ruined.

CHICHIKOV: Infinite as the sands of the sea are human passions, Excellency.

SECRETARY: Infinite indeed. He played cards, drank and squandered everything away, naturally. Your employer's estate could not be in a worse state and you want to mortgage souls to the guardians at 200 roubles a head! Who will accept him as security?

CHICHIKOV: Why be so harsh, Excellency? The estate has been ruined by cattle fever, bad harvests and a corrupt steward.

SECRETARY: Hm!

CHICHIKOV (*Taking out a bribe and giving it to the Secretary*): I believe you dropped this.

SECRETARY: I am not the only one. There are others on the board.

CHICHIKOV: They will not be forgotten. I too have been in public service. I know how matters go.

SECRETARY: Very well, give me the papers.

CHICHIKOV: The fact is, however, you should know that half the peasants are dead, so there is no difficulty later.

SECRETARY (*Laughs*): What an estate! Not only is it ruined but the people are dead.

CHICHIKOV: Well, Excellency . . .

SECRETARY: Well, according to the inspector's report they were counted as living.

CHICHIKOV: Counted as living?

SECRETARY: What are you afraid of? One dies, another is born, everything fits. As they are declared as living in the official report, they must be alive.

CHICHIKOV: Ah . . .

SECRETARY: What?

CHICHIKOV: Nothing.

SECRETARY: Well then. Hand over the papers. (*Exit*)

CHICHIKOV: Oh! I'm just a dumb idiot. I'm looking for what's right under my nose! I buy all the people who have died before the next official census . . . If I buy, say, a thousand and then mortgage them to the board at 200 roubles a head, I have a capital of 200,000. But you cannot buy or mortgage anything without land. (*Inspired*) But I buy them and move them. In Kherson they give you land free, provided you put people on it. I will move all the dead there. To Kherson, the lot of them! They can live there in peace. Now is the right time. Not long ago there was an epidemic, people died, thank God, many of them. I'll pretend to be looking for somewhere to live and try to find any nook or cranny where I can buy the people I need without too much trouble and cheaply. First, I must go and see the Governor. It will be difficult and wearisome. It is frightening to think what might happen because of this. Arrest, a public flogging and then Siberia. But man was given a brain for a reason. And the best thing is that no one will believe it. The whole thing is so unbelievable, no one will believe it. I am on my way!

(*Blackout*)

After a series of catastrophes in his life, Chichikov is, once again, back where he started, but this time, apparently without a hope in the world. There's a noose around his neck. He has taken on a very doubtful business, mortgaging a totally ruined estate on which half the people are dead. To do that, he has to go through the Secretary to the Board of Guardians, a first-rate scoundrel who can't be twisted around anyone's little finger. Chichikov has already annoyed him by his persistence. The opportunities for bribery are becoming more and more limited. But a man who is threatened by total bankruptcy and poverty is ready for anything. So Chichikov tracks the Secretary like a bloodhound in the evening and finds him at the inn. He decides that it will be either death or glory.

All this was discussed with Stanislavski as a starting point for Chichikov's behaviour in the Prologue.

'So, what would you do in the given circumstances?'

'I think that here Chichikov feels . . .'

'Don't think about that, think about what he does. So?'

Pause.

'You have your fellow actor, Vsevolod Alekseevich, in front of you. You need to get an important answer from him. Above all, try to be at ease with him. Look in his eyes and see what you can rely on, don't think, try to act instantly.'

After a few tries when something seemed to be happening, Stanislavski continued: 'But what if he refuses to listen to you and leaves? . . . Vsevolod Alekseevich, leave, don't listen to him, don't pay him any attention and you, Toporkov, stop him, not with your hands, not with any kind of physical force, but don't let him go. No, that way he will.'

'I don't know what I'm supposed to do.'

'In life, if you really needed to stop him, you would, so why can't you do it now? It couldn't be simpler. Do a very simple exercise. The task for one of you is suddenly to get up from your chair and go to that door, the task for the other is to nip his intention in the bud and stop him, preventing him from getting beyond a certain point. It's really very simple. But don't try to perform, be genuinely, naturally involved in what you are doing.'

I knew this exercise from our previous work on *The Embezzlers*.

I won't list all the subtleties of Stanislavski's teaching, as he tried to get living, organic behaviour from me in this scene, I will only say that our work was long, painstaking and only concerned physical behaviour: how to hide near to the table so the other actor can't see you, but you can observe him, as you sit almost right behind him; how to stop him dead in his tracks, block his way to the door, and how to slip him the bribe so that nobody sees, etc., etc. We were not concerned with the script.

'Now you have learned to perform a sequence of physical actions. Put them together in an unbroken line and you have the pattern of physical actions for the Prologue. What, basically, must you be able to do? Wait in ambush and watch the other actor's tiniest movements. As soon as he tries to leave, stop him, skilfully block his way, gain his interest somehow, confuse him, muddle him, and slip him the bribe so that no one else sees. That is enough for the moment. This is the first part of the way and extremely important. Find the way of doing it. If you need words, all right, but don't use the exact words in the script, only the thoughts they express. Don't do any acting, just behave. And not for us, but for the other actor. Use him to check whether your behaviour is right.'

In the second half of the Prologue leading to Chichikov's long speech that begins 'Oh! I'm just a dumb idiot', Stanislavski once again discovered a sequence of physical actions, despite the fact that all Chichikov does, apparently, is sit at the table and say his lines.

'This is not a speech, it is dialogue. There is a fierce debate between reason and feeling. Distinguish between the two. One is in the head, the other somewhere in the solar plexus. Let them speak to each other. Depending on who gets the upper hand, Chichikov either tries to jump up from the table and run away before anyone realises he is going to carry out his plan, or he uses all his strength to make himself stay sitting where he is, at the table. You're aware, you understand these impulses to action, so try to act them out.'

For the time being, everything revolved around pure physical action. We used various approaches in studying them and perfecting them, and the array of actions was significantly greater and more varied than in our work on *The Embezzlers*. Work sometimes took the form of entertaining games, sometimes of exercises, sometimes of classes where we worked on the elements of the simplest physical actions and where Stanislavski turned into the most pedantic, niggling teacher, and sometimes by narrating the whole sequence of the characters' behaviour in the Prologue. This work continued until such time as we had performed the task we had been set more or less satisfactorily, and we could narrate and perform the pattern of physical actions with ease.

At that time I still had not grasped the full significance of this type of work. I didn't know the meaning of Stanislavski's secret, that by truthfully performing physical actions and following their logic and sequence you can achieve the most complex feelings and experiences, those qualities which we had tried unsuccessfully to achieve in the first period of our work. For the moment, neither Stanislavski nor the cast spoke or thought of anything above the ordinary. We worked on solving the simplest dramatic problems and tried to work them out as perfectly as possible. And almost imperceptibly, step by step, we came to the moment when we needed the author's script, when we wanted to speak it. And there I was standing in front of the Secretary saying: 'As you wish, Excellency, but I am not leaving here until I get an answer.'

Suddenly a few claps and Stanislavski's gentle, apologetic voice: 'I am so very sorry, but I don't understand what it was you said.'

'As you wish, Excellency, but I am not leaving here until I get an answer.'

'What's that? "As you wish"?'

'As you wish, Excellency, but I am not leaving here . . .'

'No, I'm sorry, forgive me, I just don't understand . . . Hm . . . hm . . . perhaps it's my ears. I'm beginning to be hard of hearing.' He turned to his assistants. 'What does it say in the script?' The assistants tried to say the line with the utmost clarity but Stanislavski still looked blank. I even began to feel sorry for him and, using the most delicate vocal nuances, very expressively I said: 'As you wish, Excellency, but I am not leaving here until I get an answer.'

'Now I understand. Speak that clearly to the Secretary. You have to convince someone who doesn't want to listen to you. You see how dynamic you have to be in all your actions? So, go on.'

I repeated the line.

'That was awful! You're stressing every word. "*As you wish, Excellency*, but I *am* not leaving *here* until *I get an answer*." The sentence loses any kind of action. The sense would be clearer if the line, however long it may be, only had one stress. That's how you said the line to me just now. Why was that? Because you had a real wish for me to understand what you were thinking, but now you've started playacting, not behaving. Do it again, please. Awful! . . . Where's the stress in the line? "Anatomise" the sentence. Which is the one word you can't do without to express what you want from the man you are talking to? Or what is the one single word in this scene that will make you understood?

....

'What are you asking him for? What must he do to satisfy you? It's in the line! What are you thinking about? You say you won't leave this place until . . . what?'

'Until I get . . .'

'And?'

'An answer.'

'Yes, that's the important stress word. So give the sentence one single stress on that word.'

I spoke the line trying to give just one stress.

'Why are you running all the other words into one? You mustn't rush them or squash them all together, just don't stress them. So!'

I say the line again.

'Why do you hit the last word like that?'

' "Hit"?'

'Why do you hit "answer"?'

'But that's where the stress is!'

'But you don't have to hit it so hard. All you have to do is not stress the other words and then it will be a natural stress. So!'

Often, when the 'uninitiated' were present at highly difficult moments in Stanislavski's rehearsals, it seemed to them that this was all overdone, that it was actors going too far again. You can't harry people like that. And then, where is personal creativity? Worrying an actor like that can't do any good, it can only muddle him. Indeed, after working for two or three hours on one sentence you usually feel you've stopped understanding what the words mean. But it is only temporary. Afterwards, the meaning of the sentence and the words becomes very clear and having gone through this 'purifying fire' you feel a particular respect for a line that cost you so much effort. You don't gabble it, you don't overload it with unnecessary stresses, you don't 'hit' it so hard. It is real for you, musical.

Can an actor be individually so self-demanding? Can he work that relentlessly on perfecting his technique? No, since he cannot see or hear himself or recognise his faults. The bad habits that have built up over the years stick fast. He needs great patience, courage and the help of an outside person who understands the laws of the creative process. That is why we never complained when Stanislavski was so extremely exacting in rehearsals. The cultural ethos of the Moscow Art Theatre would never have come into being if the actors had not undergone his rigorous training.

But, to return to the rehearsals. Stanislavski considered action to be the sole, the indisputable basis of acting. He ruthlessly excluded everything else.

'Why are you doing that? What does it contribute to the through-action? Anything that does not lead to the accomplishment of our goal, the supertask, is superfluous. Every physical action must be dynamic, and lead to the accomplishment of some goal or other, and that includes every line you speak on stage.' He often added the dictum: 'Then your words will not be empty or your silences mute.'

Stanislavski had many ways of teaching us how to mobilise words and give the verbal action more edge. They all fell into two categories. One was to follow the external line, to study the logical construction of the sentence; the other was to follow the inner line, to make the actor develop the right mental images and pictures behind the dialogue. I have already given an example of the outer line ('As you wish, Excellency . . .'). There, Stanislavski ensured that the actor only made one stress in a long sentence, the last one, so making it dynamic and active.

'You have been give a role that consists of ideas – from 1 to 1813. All your ideas lead to the 1813th and take their colour from it.'

The actor's task in verbal action is to convey his inner images to the other actor. To do that, he has to visualise what he is talking about so clearly that he makes the other actor sees the picture he is creating with his 'inner eye' clearly and in detail.

After verbal action and the inner images that lie behind it, we had to tackle the second half of the Prologue and Chichikov's concluding speech. 'Oh! I'm a dumb idiot . . .' etc. I remember that I ran the speech very jauntily, and, for effect, banged my hand on the table on the final words, 'I am on my way', got up, moved away from the table and glanced triumphantly at Stanislavski.

'Hm! . . . Hm! . . . Dear boy, you don't see anything . . .'

???

'You're saying words. You're seeing letters, how they are printed on the page, not what Chatski sees beyond them.'

He meant to say Chichikov but absent-mindedly said Chatski,[1] which baffled me completely.

'I don't understand.'

'For example, you say, "Arrest, a public flogging and then Siberia." You understand that (here he called Chichikov, Khlestakov[2]) . . . behind these words you see pictures of an execution, a flogging, a break in the journey, the harshness of Siberia . . . That's the most important. So, do it again.'

'Oh! I'm a dumb idiot . . .'

---

[1] The main character in Griboiedov's *Woe from Wit*.
[2] The main character in Gogol's *The Inspector General*.

'You're not seeing anything, you're saying words. Find your images, see yourself as a dumb idiot, then curse yourself for being such a fool. But who is this dumb idiot? How do you see him? So, please.'

'Oh! I'm . . .'

'Awful! Hm! Instant high voltage. You're trying to work yourself up externally, to create nervous tension, and you fog the whole issue. You should simply concentrate, see clearly where your mistakes lie and curse yourself roundly. That's all it needs.

So!

'Oh! . . .'

'Why "Oh!", Not "Oh!" but "Oh! I'm a dumb idiot." Which is the stress word? If there's a false stress it means you're not seeing what you're talking about.'

And here we had the all too familiar crisis in rehearsal.

Finally, the opening of the play, the Prologue, began to emerge out of the chaos of the rough work we had done on individual moments, the overall scheme of things. It was then clear to me that Stanislavski wanted the play to begin with powerful, resonant chords and that was what he was trying to get us to do. It was important to him that all our actions should have incisive rhythms. He knew that couldn't be achieved quickly, it had to grow inside the actor, you had to establish the right pathways, the channels through which an actor's energy can flow. When this work was more or less complete, Stanislavski was able to talk about 'the result'.

'The Prologue, which we are now rehearsing,' he said, 'sets the tone for the entire play. You realise what a responsibility that is? So, what does the scene require? Attention, concentration, clear inner images and a feeling of truth, nothing more. From your table you watch the Secretary to the Board of Guardians, so as not to let him leave the inn. Your life depends upon it . . . Are you aware of the rhythm, the thoughts you need, how ready you must be at any given moment to leap thirty or forty feet to block his path? Try this simple physical action . . . so the first words you address to him – "I am not leaving here" – convey this image to him so that he clearly sees that you will create a scene in the inn if he continues to move. "I am not leaving here." Do you see what that means?

'Afterwards, when you have succeeded in making him talk to you, you have to contrive a way to give him the bribe without anyone in the inn noticing, so that if he wants to make trouble and tries to put the blame on you, it will be easier to deny it. Above all, you have to act quickly since your "employer is leaving tomorrow". When the drop of poison falls on the ready soil of Chichikov's mind, he must decide to embark on this highly risky undertaking without losing a second. That's when you most need your inner images . . . You understand? On the one hand a public flogging . . . chains . . . Siberia . . . And, on the other, 200,000 roubles, a rich estate . . . A wife, children, a family, heaven on earth, what you have striven for all your life. It's now or never, that is what you must see, and see with absolute clarity, so whichever way you choose, it will be inwardly justified and your decision will be fully rounded.'

I can't say that even after the very clear way this had been presented to us, we were able to carry it through, or that it did not present difficulties. But there was no doubt about what we had to do and what we had to work on. I could understand now why this or that moment did or didn't work, and what I had to do to make it work. I saw the boundless possibilities for an actor in this short and possibly not very significant scene. I had no doubt at all that this was so. But so much effort . . .

'Nothing is achieved without effort, only that which is achieved through effort is of value,' Stanislavski said.

At the Governor's

The next scene immediately after the Prologue is entitled *Chichikov at the Governor's*. If in the Prologue Chichikov did no more than decide to go into action, in this scene the action has already begun, he is carrying out his plan.

AT THE GOVERNOR'S

GOVERNOR (*In a dressing gown, with the medallion of St Anne round his neck, is sitting at an embroidery frame, singing*):

'Tis true a maiden young
Must not too candid be.
She may not love too openly
And she must hold her tongue.

SERVANT: Excellency, collegiate counsellor Pavel Ivanovich Chichikov is here to see you.

GOVERNOR: Chichikov? My coat! (*Sings*)

Frankly let me say to you

Old men in love are foolish.

(*The servant gives him his coat*) Show him in. (*Exit the servant*)

CHICHIKOV (*Entering*): Having arrived in the town, I counted it my prime duty to pay my respects to its leading dignitaries, and to present myself in person to Your Excellency.

GOVERNOR: I am very pleased to meet you. Do sit. (*Chichikov sits*) Where have you been employed?

CHICHIKOV: I began in the Treasury then my career continued in various places. I was on the board of construction . . .

GOVERNOR: Of what?

CHICHIKOV: The church of Christ the Saviour in Moscow, Excellency.

GOVERNOR: The right sort.

CHICHIKOV: It was a splendid opportunity. I also served in the law courts and in customs.

GOVERNOR: In customs?

CHICHIKOV: I am but a miserable worm in this world below. But I am patient, I am indeed patience personified. As to the enemies in my office, who made an attempt on my life, neither words, nor pictures, nor brush can describe them. My life can be compared to a ship in a stormy sea, Your Excellency.

GOVERNOR: A ship?

CHICHIKOV: A ship, your excellency.

GOVERNOR: He's an educated man!

CHICHIKOV: The governor's a fool!

GOVERNOR: Where do you intend to go?

CHICHIKOV: I am going to find some little spot where, in my declining years, I can spend the rest of my days. But what remains remains but to see the light and the whirling world is, so to speak, a living book and a second science.

GOVERNOR: True, true.

CHICHIKOV: To come into your province, Excellency, is like entering paradise.

GOVERNOR: Why so?

CHICHIKOV: The roads are smooth as velvet. (*The Governor smiles in embarrassment*) Provinces which appoint wise officials merit great praise.

GOVERNOR: My dear . . . Pavel Ivanovich?

CHICHIKOV: Pavel Ivanovich, Excellency.

GOVERNOR: Let me invite you to a reception I am giving today.

CHICHIKOV: I regard your invitation as a great privilege. I have

the honour to take my leave. Ah, who has embroidered this
border so delicately?

GOVERNOR *(Modestly)*: I am embroidering a purse.

CHICHIKOV: Really! *(He admires it)* I have the honour . . . *(Exit)*

GOVERNOR: Decent sort of chap. *(Sings)*

    Frankly let me say to you

    Old men in love are foolish.

(Blackout)

'How is this a link in the long chain of Chichikov's through-
action? What precise task does he set himself when visiting the
Governor? You must be clear about it so that you can then decide
how to carry it out. What actions will best enable him to achieve
his goal?'

I'll omit the narrative work we did on this scene at the table and
will go directly to the end result which we achieved in the
following way.

This visit was extremely important for Chichikov. First, at the
Governor's house he can meet the landowners from whom he can
later buy his 'goods', and also the officials he can use to complete
the formalities. But more important than just meeting them, it is
essential that it should be the Governor who introduces him into
this circle, that he should have his recommendation. But if this is
to happen, what must Chichikov achieve during his short visit?

'State it in one word. Define it with a verb that will intensify
your line of action.'

'To please the Governor.'

'Yes, but be more precise.'

'To flatter him.'

'But might we not say to win him over, to win his heart . . . You
understand?'

'Yes.'

'And what tangible signs will indicate that you have achieved
your goal one hundred per cent, so that you can feel satisfied?'

Pause.

'Did you receive anything from the Governor during your visit
that helped your through-action.'

'Yes.'

'What?'

'He was kind to me. He smiled and shook hands . . .'

'As your host he may just have been pretending.'

....

'What was it you wanted? Why did you want to gain entry to his home?'

'To meet landowners and . . .'

'And how are you going to get inside? What must you have? 'An invitation . . .'

'And did you get one?'

'Yes, he said, "Let me invite you to a reception I am giving." '

'That's most important, the most concrete thing you achieved during your visit. That's what the scene is about. Make everything lead up to it. That is what you want. Your task is: to get an invitation . . . So, what are you going to do?'

'I will speak very humbly to him.'

'But then he'll say, "What a crawler he is!" and he will dismiss you in three minutes flat. To make any tactic work, you have to have a clear idea of the person you are dealing with. That's the essential moment, when you home in on, get the feel of the other person, but you made an instant decision . . . You're seeing the Governor for the first time and the first thing you must do, if you don't want to put your foot in it, is decide quickly who the man before you is, and how best to approach him. You can only make a confident attack in the second part of your conversation. Your first action in this scene is quickly to home in on, size up the object of your attention. That's what we always do in life and never do on stage. So, let's begin.'

'I'm not sure what to do exactly. Say the lines?'

'I don't need the lines, do something.'

'But the other character . . .'

'I'll play the scene with you.'

....

'So, go out into the corridor and come back in as though it were for the first time. Behave in such as way as to make a favourable impression on me.'

'But the dialogue?'

'What do you want the dialogue for? Let's talk about our own affairs. It's your behaviour that matters to me.'

Gruelling work then began in the same spirit as in the Prologue.

'So, what are you thinking about? In life, has your task ever been to ingratiate yourself with someone?'

'Yes, but it never worked.'

'Why?'

'Because you think one thing and do another.'

'But if you did what you thought, would it work?'

'Yes, it might . . .'

'So do that. Previously, shyness inhibited you, now there's nothing to hold you back, so, please.'

Step by step we studied the nuances in the behaviour of a guest who wants to make a favourable impression on his host – the specially quiet way of coming through the door, the awestruck look in the presence of an important host, the high regard for his opinions and modesty in one's own behaviour, the respectful attitude to the objects in the room (antiques) and the well-considered, sensible, reliable answers to questions, etc. But most important, everything must be sincere, there must not be the tiniest false note which would reveal Chichikov's true nature. An audience that had not seen the Prologue would really take Chichikov for a decent, modest fellow, but one that had would be astonished at the skill of this swindler.

'But what about his character, his manner. What I do isn't Chichikov.'

'Hold on a moment. In our work we must always start with ourselves, our own personality and then follow the laws of the creative process. What of Chichikov's manner? Practise thoroughly what you are doing now and, once you can do it easily, skilfully and purposefully, you are already near to the character.'

'But Gogol has described a special bow Chichikov has . . .'

'And?'

'I can't make it work.'

'Have you practised it?'

'Yes, I tried to do it but didn't succeed.'

'Find an appropriate exercise . . . For example, mentally place a drop of mercury on the top of your head and let it roll down your back right down to your heel so that it doesn't then fall on the floor. Do this exercise several times daily. So, try . . . Awful! You're bent in two and stiff as a board. Place the drop on your head . . . Can you feel it? Wait. Now, carefully bend your head back so that the mercury runs first down your neck . . . then further down to the lower back . . . and so on.'

' "Having arrived in the town, I counted it my prime duty to pay my respects to its leading dignitaries, and to present myself in person to Your Excellency." '

'Hm! Hm! You realise that "respects to its leading dignitaries" and "present myself in person to Your Excellency" are two ideas, key words, so that in this instance "Your Excellency" is one word. After "respects to the leading dignitaries", there's a comma, then you build the sentence up towards "present myself to Your Excellency", then full stop, the voice plummets.'

We worked painstakingly through the script in this way, and Stanislavski meticulously shaped the material for the scene with the Governor, which he saw in the following way.

On a public holiday, after lunch, the Governor is sitting in his study at an embroidery frame, happily working on a design for a purse. He feels ecstatic, and sings, out of tune, a popular song that fills the room. He heard it the day before somewhere and he is very attached to it. Suddenly the footman announces a certain Chichikov. The announcement throws the Governor into total dismay; he does not wish to forsake his favourite occupation. Should he say no? But who knows who this Chichikov might be? He has to take off his dressing gown and put on his coat . . . what can he do? Devil take the man!

'My coat! –'

The Governor already hates this Chichikov person and decides to receive him as coldly and distantly as possible. He puts on his coat, stands at his desk and adopts a grand pose.

'Enter. –'

Chichikov enters. Their eyes meet like two rapiers. That is the moment they home in on each other. 'There won't be any joking with this man, he'll show me the door at once,' Chichikov thinks, 'it will be like the army.' Chichikov bows very correctly, emphasising his deep respect, and speaks as though reporting for duty,

'Having arrived in the town, I counted it my prime duty . . . –'

The first move, apparently, is a success. Chichikov is favoured by an invitation to sit down, but he is still very circumspect in his movements. He carefully approaches the desk, moves a chair back as though unworthy to sit near such a personage, and hesitates a little before sitting on this 'antique' chair. Finally, he sits right on its edge. The Governor then asks a few questions to which Chichikov must reply modestly, clearly and respectfully, without any kind of fawning, during which time, each is weighing the other up. Each has important reasons for doing this, Chichikov particularly. His fate hangs in the balance. To the Governor it is clear that Chichikov is a loyal subject and an educated man. Chichikov realises the Governor is a fool. Each then behaves accordingly: the Governor with some consideration and respect, Chichikov with shameless flattery. The clock strikes. This reminds Chichikov that he must not take up any more of a government official's time. He rises quickly and gives an especially grateful bow for his good fortune. Now he has received his invitation to the reception, he is genuinely happy, and it is easy for him to play a little scene of being overwhelmed by the Governor's generosity of heart. He bows once more and makes for the door, but suddenly catches sight of the embroidery frame. He immediately realises whose it is and lingers by it almost coincidentally. Then he silently acts out another little scene. He approaches it with a little more interest and is amazed by this work of art. He cannot seem to tear his eyes away from it. He forgets the Governor is there, forgets all courtesy, he is so astonished, frozen to the spot. Finally, after a long pause, he drags his eyes away and, bewildered, looks at the Governor.

'Who embroidered this border so beautifully?'

'I did . . . I'm embroidering a purse . . .'

Chichikov is dumbfounded. He opens his mouth in astonishment, overwhelmed, and awkwardly goes out through the door looking alternately at the design and at the genius who created it.

'Decent sort of chap!' the Governor decides, and returns to his embroidery and his song.

Stanislavski's directing turned an insignificant little scene, purely one of exposition, into something sharp-edged, meaningful and intriguing, full of humour and philosophical observation. In the scene, there is a beginning, a middle and an end: the Governor who meets Chichikov with hostility takes leave of him as a friend; Chichikov, who had thought the Governor would be a dragon, leaves thinking him a warm-hearted fool he can twist round his little finger. And every phase in the development of their relationship is crystal clear, logical, justified, it has a sequence and so is convincing. But it is one thing to plan a scene in your head and another to get a vital, organic performance out of it, so that you have living people, not actors, on stage.

Stanislavski had long since understood that the basic secret in mastering a role lies above all in studying the character's physical behaviour. If that is truthful, and engages you, then it will be easy and natural to find the speech patterns.

I remember a story the actress Stepanova[1] told about the first time she worked with Stanislavski. She was still a young actress, of about sixteen or seventeen,[2] and had just joined the company. She had immediately been cast as Mstislavskaya in *Tsar Fiodor*[3] and was called for rehearsal that very same day. It was useless trying to learn the part. There was simply no time. Stepanova went to the theatre, hid terrified in a corner and awaited her fate. They got to her scene. Stanislavski asked, 'Who's playing Mstislavskaya?' The young actress shyly stepped forward and was introduced to Stanislavski. He greeted her warmly and asked her to go on stage and rehearse.

'But I don't know what to do. I haven't learned the lines.'

'I'm very glad you haven't. Put down your script and go into the garden to meet your young man . . . he will climb over the fence to you. Wait for him . . . listen carefully, try to guess which direction he will appear from. When he jumps over the fence, play some sort of game with him, hide, frighten him. Can you do that? Start . . .'

'But what do I say?'

'Whatever you want in the given circumstances.'

I remember other moments in my career. A few days before the season ended, I went to see Stanislavski to take my leave before the break. That was when we were in the thick of our work on *Dead Souls*.

'How should I work on the role during the break?' I asked before we parted.

'Leave the role and the script behind. Take a rest, but in your free time plan all kinds of swindles. Choose a victim from among your neighbours and work out down to the last detail how you could cheat him, how you would get to know him, how you would gain his confidence. That especially. That's Chichikov's strength, gaining his victim's confidence. Your plan must be very precise

[1] Angelina Stepanova, one of the great stars of the Moscow Art Theatre, joined the company in 1924. She was still performing well into her eighties.

[2] She was, in fact, nineteen.

[3] A historical drama by Aleksei Tolstoy, the first play ever to be presented by the Moscow Art Theatre, in 1898.

and detailed. And you must plan everything as though you were really going to carry it out. When you have worked out one plan, think up another for another neighbour with a different character, income and position. He is different, so the plan will be completely different. Once you have solved this problem, pass on to the next, always asking the question: If I needed to deceive this particular man, with this particular personality, living in such and such a place . . . etc. If I had to rob him, say, what would I do under these circumstances? When you come back after the break, you can tell me a whole series of interesting cases of clever "robberies" you have committed. That will be of great use to you in mastering the role of Chichikov. I wish you luck. Goodbye, and have a rest.'

Some particularly conscientious and dedicated actors arrive at the first rehearsal word perfect. That delights directors of the old school, but it would have worried Stanislavski. He was terrified of letting an actor say the lines too soon. The danger, for him, was that the lines lay in 'the muscles of the tongue'. The way the lines were spoken should not be the result of muscular training. That would inevitably make them empty, cold, wooden. They would mean nothing, and be set for ever. This was inevitable, too, if the actor didn't first prepare the other, complex, aspects of his creative apparatus, and started by working on the script itself. On the other hand, the lines would always be living, organic, clear, if they were the result of genuine intentions, needs, clear inner images, clear thoughts, out of which a character can be created. It was to these factors that an actor should pay attention when working on a role.

At one rehearsal for *Tartuffe*, Stanislavski said: 'First of all, you must establish the logical sequence of your physical actions. That's how you should start working. Work based on the muscles of the tongue is hack work, but when an actor has inner images, it is creative work.'

At Manilov's

The scene with Manilov proved very difficult and, at first, impossible to play. The problem was we couldn't define the main character's line of action. What Gogol has written is very engaging, clear and all-embracing, but how is it to be translated into the language of the stage, how can we actively express Manilov's inactivity?

Mikhail Kedrov, later to become a director, who was playing the role, saw more clearly than anyone else that he could not create a whole character until he had defined, precise, active tasks. But it was extremely difficult to find these tasks, to hear, as it were, the character breathing. Kedrov could not answer the question: What does Manilov want? What does he want with all his heart when he receives Chichikov? The explanations Sakhnovski offered were to do with the story, who Manilov was, and, of course, could not satisfy a demanding actor trying to get his performance on the right track. The exchanges between Kedrov and the director dragged on and on, so that he gave the impression of being stubborn and wilful.

'What is it you don't understand?' Sakhnovski asked.

'Everything.'

'Everything? I simply don't know what to say to you.'

'Tell me what he wants . . .'

'How can he want anything? He's a nothing, a blank in the human race.'

'That doesn't give me anything. How can he not want something? He says, "In that case, Pavel Ivanovich, I invite you to sit in this armchair. This chair is specially reserved for guests."'

'And?'

'He wants him for some reason to sit in the specially reserved chair.'

'Oh, God! This is impossible! On the whole, he's sentimental and . . . .'

'I know who he is. Gogol has told us that already. I want you to tell me how I'm supposed to play it. Look, they have just got up from the table after their meal. Manilov invites Chichikov to eat some more, but he refuses, and asks for a little time to talk business. Manilov invites him into his study, sits him in a comfortable chair, offers him a pipe and in a long reverie, full of compliments, pours out his joy at having Chichikov in his home, dreams of sharing a life with him "in the shade of an elm tree" and so on. What's this all about? It's all so "in general". He entertains him in general, he makes him sit in general, he dreams in general. Where's the hidden purpose in all this, what is his through-action? You can only decide how to do it in the light of this . . .'

'For heaven's sake, what purpose can he possibly have?! He has no purpose.'

'That can't be. Then there'd be nothing to act, nobody would listen.'

This kind of discussion took place at every rehearsal in an infinite number of variations. I didn't at the time fully understand that Kedrov had ambitions to be a director. And even he wasn't sure about it. But he was right. You shouldn't act anything 'in general'. A clear theatrical language had to be found for the scene between Chichikov and Manilov, the language of action. Chichikov's task is crystal clear: to persuade Manilov to sell him dead souls. If the audience is to see and follow the logic of his actions, if it to is engage their interest, there must be obstacles. These obstacles arise from the logic of the other person's – Manilov's – action, but to find that logic, you need to know what he wants. And it's no use looking for these wants in the abstract. They must arise from the scene itself and be understood as the decisions the character himself makes.

It was a very difficult problem, complicated both by Manilov's character and the dramatic material itself.

If we just begin with the scene as written, Manilov can appear simply as a welcoming, gentle, even charming and generous host, whom Chichikov can talk to and easily get what he wants. That may be so. But that is only how Manilov appears at the beginning of Gogol's book. The further we go on, the worse he becomes, and in a very short time we begin to tire of him. How are we to show that on stage? What 'wants', what actions can express it?

That was the reason for Kedrov's questions, that was what he was trying to get at in rehearsal. We tried to get out of trouble by using some attractive externals, for example, in his way of standing, or speech oddities, but they were not successful. They could only be incidentals, the rest hung fire and soon became irritating.

But Kedrov's efforts and questioning were not without success. As rehearsals progressed, here and there he found answers. We started to feel that the scene could work, and could hold us. We became aware of a certain unifying logic in Manilov's behaviour, and that was good. Kedrov was on the right track, but he lacked confidence. He needed fully to understand the logic of Manilov's behaviour, to find the right words, the right verb to define it. Until he had done that, he could not shake off a feeling of insecurity, and that could not but be reflected in his attitude.

When the scene was shown to Stanislavski something curious

happened at the start. When Manilov's room had been roughly set up, and Kedrov and I had taken our places, Stanislavski said, in his usual way, 'No acting. I'm not here,' etc., and asked us to begin. But before we could open our mouths he turned to Sakhnovksi and started to whisper. We decided to wait but the conversation with Sakhnovski continued. We looked at each other, and then began quietly to discuss whether we should wait or start the scene. We went on arguing until one of us insisted that we begin but we had hardly said the first lines before we were interrupted.

'What's going on? Why this ham acting suddenly? You started so well and now we suddenly have this playacting.'

'But we hadn't begun . . .'

'Of course you had. Before you started yelling your lines you related properly to each other and that's how you should have gone on. What is the meaning of the scene? Neither Manilov nor Chichikov wants to be the first to enter the room and each defers to the other and you began this argument about who could more cleverly defer to the other very well. I was watching you the whole time although I was busy with my own conversation and suddenly you ruined everything . . . Quite awful!'

We didn't tell him what had really happened and the rehearsal continued.

'Well now, you have found a lot of truth here and lived truthfully,' said Stanislavski when the scene had ended. 'Do you know what you need now? This first purchase of dead souls is the most difficult, it is the cornerstone. Chichikov had chosen to start with Manilov because he had calculated he would be the easiest subject, but he turns out to be the most difficult. How are we to do this? What is the action and what is the counter-action? Chichikov's task is clear: but obstacles must be put in his way. Manilov must make it difficult for Chichikov to conduct his business. How do you, Kedrov, get Chichikov into the chair? Try to seat him in as uncomfortable a position as possible, admire the beauty of his pose and suffer deep despair if he tries to change it. You, Toporkov, imperceptibly try to change your position and prepare for a private conversation. You, Kedrov, watch him and either don't let him change his position or make it even more contorted. That is one element of the conflict. Try to find it.'

Stanislavski watched us do a series of exercises.

'Do you understand the difference between Manilov's and Chichikov's tasks? If Manilov were simply a cordial, hospitable, generous host, it would all be very simple. But he is in love with himself. The concern of a really cordial, generous host is the comfort of his guest. Manilov is concerned with his own comfort and tortures his guest. He is interested in staging an event: "Chichikov and I are at table eating", "We are sitting in armchairs and talking philosophy", "Chichikov and I are dreaming of life under the same roof", etc., etc., and so all his concerns for his guest are the concerns of a photographer arranging a group photograph. Do you see how this might try one's patience? Even Chichikov's, who has come to discuss a dangerous and ticklish business. Try to do something like that.'

We liked the task. There was something to get our teeth into. We began. As we developed the idea Stanislavski had given us, we became more and more involved in our improvisation, and created a series of vivid, comic moments, and, most important of all, we felt we had something solid to rely on, we understood what the clash, the argument, the conflict was.

'You see what it's about? Chichikov, who has come on very delicate, complicated business, finds a man whose task is to use his arrival to take a whole series of "photographs" on the theme "Chichikov on my estate". You see how different your tasks are, and how each of you prevents the other from getting what he wants? It is difficult for Chichikov to overcome the obsessed "photographer", who is creating his sentimental head-in-the-clouds "photographs", and bring him down to earth, and, on the other hand, the difficulty of Manilov's task to make the dead souls, who have unexpectedly emerged, part of his "photographs".

'Each of you must bring great force and energy to his tasks. Chichikov can hardly control his anger, but has to be polite and tactful, and work out an ingenious strategy so he can take control of the conversation. And later on, when the fatal words have been spoken and Manilov is speechless with surprise, he has to decide whether or not he is dealing with a madman. Chichikov needs enormous effort and ingenuity to bring Manilov to his senses and persuade him that the business of the dead souls will finally cement their friendship. Once persuaded, Manilov is ablaze with enthusiasm, and thinks of creating an idyllic group photograph in which his wife and children will take part. Chichikov then encounters his most difficult task, to get out of Manilov's house come what may, and Manilov's task is to die rather than let him go. You understand the rhythm here? Your acting is very limp.

We need passion here. Try the beginning of the scene. Chichikov gets up from the table, very full, but the Manilovs want to make him eat something more ... No, they don't ask, what I said was make him, *make* him, force him, press him. You can create a whole scene out of this, and then there is the argument about who is to go into the study first, etc., etc. Chichikov leaves Manilov's home bathed in sweat. Have you understood all that?'

'Yes, of course.'

'Then try it, but don't imagine you have really understood until you can actually do it properly.'

Of course, there was a great deal more to do, but Stanislavski's precise, concrete direction had opened up the way for us to get on top of this difficult material, and there was the tantalising thought that we might be able to bring Gogol's characters vividly to life.

At Nozdriov's

Stanislavski often held private meetings with the other directors in which he discussed their work with them and showed them the way they should go. After one of these meetings, we asked Sakhnovski what they had discussed the day before. At first he hesitated a little, but then gave us the substance of Stanislavski's thoughts. Basically, the discussion came down to his making a series of critical remarks about the actors and the direction the play was taking, and then his indicating a number of weak spots, with suggestions as to how to improve them. And all his comments were concerned with the acting. For him, the only way to make Gogol's novel flesh and blood was through the subtlety and richness of the acting.

'In every scene I need a set that doesn't distract, but allows me to see the actors' eyes. We don't need moves. When Plyushkin and Chichikov are sitting opposite each other and talking, all that interests me is their eyes.'

In fact, in his search for the right set, Stanislavski rejected two versions of a design by Dmitriev and only accepted a third by Simov[1] as a compromise, but was still not entirely happy. When he rejected Dmitiriev's first version, Stanislavski gave the following advice: that in the acting area itself, that is the place where the

[1] Simov was the first young designer Stanislavski ever worked with in the early years of the Moscow Art Theatre.

scene takes place (and it must always be limited), everything must be perfect and real, but the further away you move away from the centre, the less distinct everything becomes, rather like a charcoal drawing, a background, a grey wall. The decor must seem like a sketch. The model had looked quite appealing, and it seemed as though it would be all right. But once it was set up and the actors came on, it was obvious that it would be a distraction. The design was then handed over to Simov, who suggested a series of neutral drapes which covered all the unnecessary parts of the set and left only the acting area free. This principle was applied in the performance.

Stanislavski was absolutely insistent about the way to work with actors.

'You see, Sakhnovski, you are very good at "demonstrating" to actors. You, undoubtedly, have talent. You should try to act. But "demonstrating" to actors seldom gets you very far. You have to lure them with the right "bait". That is the art of the teacher-director. There are actors of great imagination, and all you have to do is point them in the right direction, and there are actors whose imagination needs to be stirred all the time for them to develop and grow. Don't confuse these two types, or apply the same method to them. You mustn't give an actor ready-made solutions. Your job is to lure them with the right kind of "bait". You just have to be aware of what will tempt him and under what circumstances.'

Stakhnovski tried not to leave out anything Stanislavski had said and ended with the words: 'I think I've told you everything. Now forget it. Stanislavski was anxious that we shouldn't say anything.'

This remarkable ability Stanislavski had to find the right bait, to stir the actor's imagination and his creative forces, enabled him sometimes to create inspirational moments in rehearsal. I remember a rehearsal of the scene between Chichikov and Nozdriov – a vivid, energetic scene in which two crooks meet. This is Chichikov's first failure, and it has dire consequences. Moskvin played Nozdriov with his usual humour and verve. This scene went much more easily for me than others had. We were managing it well even before Stanislavski saw it. It was very watchable, and we were very anxious to show it, hoping for his full approval. But the presentation was put off for quite trivial reasons. The scene went well, it had tension, but at the end there is a game of draughts that Nozdriov plays with Chichikov. During the whole game they exchange the same phrases. One says, 'It's a long time since I played draughts.' 'We all know how badly you play,' replies the other.

That game ruined everything. It brought a scene that had been going smoothly to a complete halt. We didn't know what to do to stop this game blocking the forward drive of the scene. Nozdriov is entertaining Chichikov and is trying to get him drunk so that he can then get him involved in some shady deal. Chichikov refuses any more drink, as he is just about ready to broach the business of buying dead souls. Nozdriov, sensing that his guest has something to propose to him, gets rid of his brother-in-law and is left face to face with Chichikov. The two crooks begin to angle for each other. No sooner has Nozdriov heard Chichikov's wish to buy 'dead souls' than he showers him with suggestions as to how it can be done: he offers them as a gift, provided he buys a stallion very cheap, or some filly or other, or a dog, a puppy, etc. Or he suggests exchanging them for a carriage or to 'wager' for them. Chichikov rejects all these suggestions, enraging Nozdriov. Finally, offended by the abuse that has been heaped on him, he thinks about escaping from Nozdriov's clutches and leaving his property. But not so. Nozdriov, the compulsive gambler, cannot let his victim go so easily. He suggests a game of draughts.

'This isn't cards, which is nothing but cheating. This needs brains.'

Chichikov lets himself be drawn, because he knows how good he is at this game. He sits down to play, betting one hundred roubles against Nozdriov's dead souls.

Up to that moment the scene had been very tight, not very subtle perhaps, but it had excitement, energy, charm and good humour. But at soon as we sat down to play – stop. The end of the scene was limp, and destroyed all the work we had done earlier.

We tried everything: making the scene shorter and faster, 'dressing up' certain moments in the game with funny tricks, varying the way we said lines, adlibbing and, finally, cutting it altogether. But we weren't happy with any of it. Our failure in this part of the scene made us put off showing it to Stanislavski. We wanted to find our own solution, and then show the scene in all its glory. Unfortunately, nothing worked and we had to show the scene as it was. Perhaps, we thought, it would somehow come right; if not, he would find the answer.

'So, did you think the scene came off or not?' Stanislavski asked after we had shown it to him.

'Shouldn't we cut the game of draughts?'

'Why?'

'It ruins everything. We tried it all ways but it didn't work. It's difficult to play. It seems superfluous. Pointless.'

'The game of draughts is the most important moment in the scene. Don't you see?'

'It holds up the rhythm.'

'Does it, indeed! This is the tensest moment in the entire scene. Suddenly . . . the rhythm is ferocious.'

'We don't understand. They sit and move the pieces . . .'

'Have you never been to a chess tournament? They sit there too, and move the pieces, but there are moments of great tension. You tell me you've worked a lot on this scene. That's good, but, evidently, not in the right direction. Tell me how you worked and what you did.'

We told him everything we could in detail.

'Hm! . . . Hm!' Pause. 'Tell me, please, how high is Chichikov's stake?'

'One hundred roubles.'

'And Nozdriov's?'

'Nozdriov? He doesn't bet anything, he is playing for the dead souls.'

'Right.' Pause. 'And how many does he have?'

'What?'

'Dead souls'

Silence.

'I am asking how many dead souls he has.'

'Well, more or less . . . it doesn't say how many . . . Probably quite a few . . . But . . . I don't know.'

'You don't know? And you, Toporkov, do you know?' he said, turning to me.

'Absolutely not.'

'Dear heaven, dear heaven! . . . what am I to do? . . . It means you . . . What have I been teaching you? Hm! . . . Hm! . . . You're going off on another tack . . . Oh dear, oh dear! We'll have to start all over again. Of course, you can't play this scene, however hard you try. You don't know the most important thing, which is, why you are gambling, how high the stakes are! It's one thing to play for a few pence, another for a whole fortune. They are different things. Before we start work, you have to know what it is you want. What would you call this scene? "Gambling fools"? Or "Gambling fever" or "Life or Death"? Or something else? You tried to play it without knowing what you were doing. It's clear your work wasn't on the right lines. You went after incidentals, tricks, not the essentials. So, think, how many dead souls does Nozdriov own?'

We spent the remaining part of the rehearsal in a lively discussion about the way landowners live, their serfs. We discussed our ideas, proposals, we read parts of *Dead Souls*. We had to determine Nozdriov's status among the landowners, estimate his wealth and roughly calculate the number of his dead souls who could be counted as living at any given moment for the census. Stanislavski led the discussion, pointing it very cleverly in the right direction, not allowing us to stray from the matter in hand.

Finally, we established the fact that Nozdriov might have two hundred dead serfs who might officially be considered living, that is, the ones that Chichikov needed. If he won them and mortgaged them to the council of guardians for two hundred roubles a head, he would get 40,000 roubles in cash.

'Do you realise now what kind of game Chichikov is playing? He risks one hundred roubles and can win 40,000 – a whole fortune. That is what you *have* to understand. You see what every move means to him, and how he would feel if he were to lose that huge sum because Nozdriov cheated! Think all this through very carefully and try to see what you would do in the given circumstances.'

With that, Stanislavski left us till our next rehearsal, which took place very soon afterwards and was exclusively devoted to the game of draughts. Stanislavski asked me a whole set of questions about gambling. He asked me if I played cards, did I ever play for large sums, win or lose a lot, how it happened, what I did when the excitement was at its peak, etc. I told him of some incidents from my past.

'Remember what the inner rhythm was at decisive moments when you were playing. Can you tell me how he behaves?'

....

'You have to win, come what may. It could be a question of

honour, of your life, whatever you like. Draughts in not a game of chance, but of brains, of calculation. How do you marshal your skills so as not to miss a golden opportunity to set up a winning combination of moves? Remember moments from your own life which would make a good story. Like when you risked a large sum in Irkutsk.'

'I felt then that . . .'

'No, I don't care about your feelings, tell me what you did. Remember.'

'I watched the way the banker looked at his cards, and I tried to guess how many high cards he had and what I should do: buy more cards or stick with five.'

'And he?'

'I thought he was watching me closely too.'

'Why do you think it was closely?'

'I could see it in his eyes.'

'What colour are Moskvin's eyes? Why do you have to look? You should know that already. How many times have you played draughts with him in rehearsal! You really can't remember the colour of his eyes?! But you can still probably remember the eyes of the man you played with in Irkutsk. What is missing now? What's been lost? Where did the passion for gambling go? The fact is, you didn't pay Moskvin, the actor you are playing with, any attention. The element of attention, close attention was missing. That's where you need to start work: train your concentration, give it things to do, develop the ability to pay attention to another actor, use simple things at first, then go on to more subtle things and then much more subtle things. Remember, if, after a scene, you can recall all the barely perceptible finer points of your partner's behaviour, it means you played the scene well, and you have the most important quality an actor needs – concentration. When you were playing cards in Irkutsk, you did that instinctively, because you were afraid that disaster would befall you if you lost. On stage, there was no real danger, but your own experience should tell you what you should do. Train yourself to do it. Are you good at draughts?'

'No, very feeble.'

'Set up the board. Start to play . . . Why did you make that move? Before making it, you should think two or three moves ahead and try to work out what Moskvin's response will be, and what position your pieces will be in after that . . . Did you guess his moves?'

'No.'

'Play some more, only think two moves ahead again and at the same time watch Moskvin's left hand. He will palm your hundred roubles from the table. Moskvin, do that, and you, Toporkov, try to cover the note before he can make the slightest move with his hand in that direction, and think above your moves . . . So, go on playing. Only play quite naturally through to the end. We'll see who's the better player . . . Eh! . . . you see, your hundred-rouble note has gone, that was lack of concentration. Concentration, concentration, concentration! . . . Moskvin, your cheating was too obvious. Chichikov would immediately refuse to play with you. You have to find the right moment . . . Play on.'

These exercises went on for a long time until there came the kind of change that can only be the result of consistent hard work in the right direction. We had really become involved in our game, we watched each other closely and so we were not at our ease in our chairs. You could feel the tension between two inveterate gamblers, their rhythm, and their pretence of outward calm as they said: 'It's a long time since I played draughts', 'We all know how badly you play', which could only underline the true feelings of two gamblers. I saw how Moskvin's eyes glittered. Subsequently this became our favourite scene in the whole play.

Our next rehearsal with Stanislavski on this scene took place much later, after *Dead Souls* had opened and was in the repertoire. But both the assistant directors and Stanislavski himself were concerned to improve it. No understudy could be rehearsed into even a minor, let alone a major, role without Stanislavski seeing him and giving his approval.

Livanov took over as Nozdriov. He was a very talented character actor, with unflagging imagination and an ebullient nature which was right for comedy. His impatience in his wish to capture the character quickly (he was also a wonderful caricaturist) always made his early work somewhat chaotic. His performance seemed confused, often superficial and external. But he was aware of it. He felt his failure deeply, and went on working until he discovered the right shape and balance. This was true of Nozdriov. The role was perfectly within his range and he liked it. He wasn't satisfied with the adaptation and he added in a number of things taken from various parts of Gogol's novel. He created a long speech about how happy he had been at the local fair, the good time he had spent with some officers, recalling a certain Lieutenant Kuvshinikov with whom he was sure Chichikov would have made friends.[1] This scene was shown to Stanislavski. Livanov, on the whole, did not play it badly, but not as well as he might. His performance lacked the genuine inner pleasure of Nozdriov's infectious personality, and was mostly external. The speech was a difficult one, demanding acting of a very high technical level.

'Well, now, dear boy, that's all right . . . more or less, but you don't really see what you are talking about. Tell me, how did you do with the officers at the fair?'

Livanov, as I have said, was a man of great imagination and told a whole series of different versions of what might have happened in the company of drunken officers.

Stanislavski half-listened to him, as though he was thinking about something else, and finally said: 'This is just childish stuff. Were they really officers? More like schoolgirls. Just imagine them all.'

Then he began to tell stories that made our jaws drop in surprise, and it was a long time before we came to our senses. We collapsed in uncontrollable laughter and had a hard time getting a grip on ourselves so that we could hear the rest of what Stanislavski was saying. In scene after vivid and colourful scene, he pictured the whole debauch, all the outrageous things the officers did at the fair, and when he described in detail what exactly Lieutenant Kuvshinikov did and how he made such an impression on Nozdriov, we fell off our chairs with laughter. How such images could come into the mind of a modest, innocent man like Stanislavski is impossible to tell, but it gave a special piquancy to his story.

When we had calmed down a little, we did the scene again and Livanov's speech sounded quite different. His eyes shone and sparkled. Everything Stanislavski had described so vividly passed before his inner eye, it came alive for him and he summoned up all his energy to find the colours with which to convey to Chichikov the enormous impression the officers' binge had made on him, and when he referred to Lieutenant Kuvshinikov, the picture Stanislavski had given him came into his mind so that he could hardly speak the word 'Lieutenant' or 'Kuvshinikov' because he was

[1] This scene underwent considerable cuts. (Toporkov's note.)

convulsed with uncontrollable laughter. He could only give free range to his feelings and laugh to his heart's content. It was living, human laughter that captured everything he felt. It was Nozdriov's infectious laughter. It was Gogol.

Rehearsals on the whole were happy. Stanislavski was in a good mood. Livanov often contributed to it. He was a very witty person, always larding his work and his talk with jokes. As here, when we finished the scene successfully, and Stanislavski turned to him and said:

'Now, dear boy, this is now simply marvellous . . . a master-piece.'

'Well, yes', answered Livanov, 'but one can't do it a second time . . .'

'Under no circumstances.'

'That's the trouble. You say it's a masterpiece, and then what? If it were, say, a picture I could sell it right away, but all we have is this "piffle".'

Stanislavski laughed long and loud, and on leaving, he calmed Livanov down with the assurance that theatre has its advantages too, but Livanov persisted with his joke, and despairingly brushed these words aside, and continued to bewail his lost masterpiece.

At Plyushkin's

During one of our rehearsals in Stanislavski's study at Leontievski Lane, the conversation turned to new trends in drama. Stanislavski, who could no longer go to the theatre, listened with great interest and attention to our accounts of productions in Moscow. We told him about the formalist contrivances of some directors, admired by some groups of the time, especially the fashionable ones, who considered them to be the avant-garde that would supplant the obsolete, academic Moscow Art Theatre.

'We must take this calmly and not lose heart,' said Stanislavski. 'We must go on perfecting our art and our technique. There are false experiments and trends which for a while seem to be the last word. They appear to threaten the foundations of realism, but they cannot destroy it entirely. Formalism is a temporary phenomenon, we must wait for it to end, but not with our hands folded, we must work. Someone must take care to protect the living shoots of real art from the weeds that try to smother it. We can be quietly confident that the moment will come when it will grow and flower. The weeds will wither, but we must protect the shoots. That is our task, difficult though it be. This is our solemn duty, our debt to art.'

His words rang out cheerfully and confidently, his eyes shone. But later, listening to an account of Shakespeare's *Hamlet* in a Moscow theatre where the wonderful character of the thinker-philosopher was played comically, and the poetic figure of Ophelia, at the director's behest, was played as a whore, Stanislavski wilted and sighing deeply, said sadly:

'That is the death of art.'

Then he started to work with great energy. That day he was especially critical of us. His demands were impossibly high. He attacked us for the least mistake or evidence of bad taste. At times he was cruel and unjust. We were paying for those who had outraged Shakespeare's genius.

An important chapter in *Dead Souls* did not fare well in the adaptation. Plyushkin is in his room. Chichikov enters and, having taken him for the housekeeper, opens up a conversation. After discovering his mistake, Chichikov disguises the real purpose of his scheme as an act of charity to the old man and, having obtained his agreement to surrender his dead souls, he leaves the miserly landowner's estate. Plyushkin was played by the well-known actor, Leonidov,[1] who had all the gifts necessary to play this character. He was an interesting man. His age, his extreme individuality, his penetrating, suspicious eye, his strong, tenor-like, almost at times 'feminine' voice, his inclination towards tragedy were guarantees that the role of Plyushkin was in good hands, and that the theatre would be able to show the deeply tragic side of a once important man, a good host and family man, eaten away by a fatal passion. But how was anyone to show all the complexities of a character so fully and lovingly and richly described in the novel? There is no way of packing the full meaning of Gogol's descriptions and poetic digressions into an adaptation. In the play, this is just a minor episode, a business discussion about the sale of dead souls, that's all. This annoyed Leonidov. He felt that there was not sufficient

---

[1] Leonid Mironovich Leonidov (1873–1941. He played Othello in the ill-fated Moscow Art Theatre production of 1930 when his interpretation was shaped by Stanislavski.

opportunity for him to give free rein to his personality and his talents.

Leonidov was always very respectful in his attitude to Stanislavski. Every rehearsal with Stanislavski was for him an exciting event. He did not wish to seem unprepared when he first showed the scene to Stanislavski, so he worked very hard and was very demanding on himself and on me. I wasn't doing very well, and he helped me in any way he could, realising that if he did not have a good Chichikov, his own part would suffer.

It was clear the scene wasn't going well. Leonidov's delivery was exceptionally clear, he conveyed certain moments of Plyushkin the miser wonderfully. But it was only interesting in places. On the whole it was rather dull and didn't hold the audience.

I'm talking about the small audience that was always present at rehearsals, and if we didn't manage to hook 'our' audience, what could we expect from an audience of unknowns who would be in the house when we were in performance. But that was some time off and, for the moment, the most important phase was to show our work to Stanislavski.

I don't think I have ever seen Stanislavski in such a concentrated mood in rehearsal as on that day, in his study, when we showed him the Plyushkin scene for the first time. All his attention was directed not towards me but towards Leonidov. My acting was feeble, I felt helpless, but he ignored me completely, I didn't exist for him. He watched Leonidov, he didn't take his eyes off him, fearing to miss his slightest movement, his breathing, his delivery. He sat stock still. You could read his thoughts from his face, at which, I confess, I glanced from time to time. Mostly, his expression was not very favourable to us.

We finished. There was a long, agonising pause.

Stanislavski took off his pince-nez and stared at a fixed spot, apparently trying to find the words for his sad diagnosis.

Leonidov waited, pale, with downcast eyes.

In my despair, I feigned total indifference and calm. The co-directors and the assistants prepared to write notes.

'Hm! . . . Hm! Very good . . . Leonidov, you've found some good things . . . (Long pause.) But it's all rather amorphous, all "in general". There is no real shape, and your moods don't work at all. There's no beginning, no development, no climax, no end in the scene. Plyushkin is a miser, try to find moments when he is kind . . . not kind but generous, a spendthrift, a rake, and make this the climax of the role. Then your miserliness will work, it will emerge clearly and powerfully in the last line of the scene, "No, I will leave it (my watch) to him after my death, so he will remember me." How do you express your miserliness? Only through the things that happen to you. But you pay little attention to them, you turn in on yourself, to your inner world. Throughout the scene you are afraid to show the miser that you are, and that's not right. You must start with what happened today. Play each moment through in detail. That's the only way you can develop the character.

'What has happened? Plyushkin has come back home after collecting the usual rubbish. He has a basketful of trash which he adds to the heap on the floor. But for Plyushkin this is not rubbish or waste, this is a rich collection of antiques. He has been absent a long time. The house has been empty and there are, in his opinion, thieves in the area. How difficult it had been to get back with his basket of treasures without being robbed! When he comes into the room he gives an anxious look round to make sure than no one has got in during his absence.

'When he is a little calmer, he settles himself beside the pile and begins to sort and count the items in his collection. That's when the curtain goes up and your scene begins.

'This is the beginning of the action. The audience sees Plyushkin and his room for the first time. Everything is of interest. You have no need to rush. You can play a big scene here, "Plyushkin surveys his treasures". Can you play that? Just that? You realise what splendid material this is for an actor? If you perform this scene in every detail, in all its human integrity, you can hold the audience in rapt attention without saying a word. But you are throwing this opportunity away, ignoring it and rushing into the dialogue with Chichikov far too soon. You think that is your salvation, but it isn't true. Before Chichikov says his first line to Plyushkin there are many events and experiences, all of which are of interest to us as an audience. We see how an old man, looking like an old woman, digs into a pile of rubbish with great concentration and lovingly inspects every object he extracts, be it a horseshoe or the sole of an old boot. He is absorbed in what he is doing and so doesn't hear the door being carefully opened by Chichikov, who comes into the room, and tries to decide whether what he sees is an old woman or a peasant. Plyushkin senses someone looking at him, and turns to Chichikov and their eyes meet. What does this mean for Plyushkin? What he has feared all is life, his constant nightmare, that a thief might sneak in on his valuables. And what a thief! Not one of those who live locally, near his estate, he knows them all; no, this is someone new, a newcomer, evidently an arch-specialist in robbery and murder.

'What is he to do? After the first moment of shock, Plyushkin takes a whole series of precautions to save his life, hiding his fear, however, from the thief so that he can trick him, leap out of the room and call for help.

'In these circumstances, it is difficult for Chichikov to start a conversation, and this mutual incomprehension, this aiming for opposite goals (one, to begin a conversation, the other to flee from the room), creates a telling theatrical moment.

'The first words are finally spoken, the situation is more or less clear and the dialogue begins.

'But you go straight into the dialogue, and leave out the most interesting thing – the moment when they home in on, latch on to each other.

'You never leave that out in life. But on stage for some reason you do. I assure you, this is very important, it is what convinces an audience the most and sets the actor on the path towards truth, a belief in what he is doing. That's the most important thing.

'Moments when you home in on someone can be short, barely perceptible, depending on the situation, but they can sometimes be the opposite. The moment when you feel each other out doesn't invariably end when the other person starts to speak. The first few words don't sound really active because neither has yet sized the other up. They continue to feel each other out, so that they can manipulate each other better. That is especially true of a suspicious person like Plyushkin.

'You see, before he works out who Chichikov is, and is convinced that he is nothing other than an angel from heaven, sent to him in gratitude for his enormous generosity and humility, he takes him for a thief or for a landowner who has come in the expectation of a good meal, or for a penniless hussar who wants money, etc. These are all moments when you home in on your object, connect, then home in again and connect again as new circumstances arise.

'The second part is: "Plyushkin realises he has found a benefactor". How can he show his gratitude, win him over so that he will continue to be benevolent? Plyushkin then arranges a "banquet". He has the samovar brought in, brings the crumbs of an Easter cake he had been given three years previously by his family. Now he is a rich landowner, a splendid host, giving an unprecedented feast. Play Plyushkin as an extravagant wastrel, forget all about his meanness, just take one task, how best to entertain your benefactor, to amaze him by the scale of your extravagance and at the same time to expedite the formalities of selling the dead souls as quickly as possible. There are two critical moments in this second half, when the whole business almost falls through. One arises from the fact that Plyushkin cannot go into the town, the other from the fact that there isn't a clean sheet of paper.

'These are crucial moments, don't rush them, play them right through.

'For Plyushkin, the lack of a clean sheet of paper is critical. The important thing is to look for one in a natural manner. Only by the way you look can you convey the depth of what you are feeling. You need great concentration, total attention. In a word, don't feel, do something.

'Finally, the obstacles are overcome and the business is concluded. Chichikov, the wonderful benefactor, has bought not only dead, but also runaway souls.

'The third part of the scene is how to thank this exceptional man adequately. He has been so kind and generous and even refused refreshment.

'The goal of the part is "To see Chichikov out". Only think of one thing, how to express your love, your respect, your gratitude to your guest. Forget all about Plyushkin's moroseness, his jaundiced grumbling, his misanthropy. Now, he is warm, he is all philanthropy. Play Afanasi Ivanovich in *The Old Time Landowners*.[1]

'And now comes the last part of the scene, "Plyushkin alone". For the first few minutes he has a lingering anxiety as to whether he has done enough to please his cherished guest. He suddenly feels that he has given him all too few marks of gratitude. He hurries to the window where he sees Chichikov getting into his carriage, he runs to the pile of rubbish, or to his desk, fighting with his desire to do something. Finally, he feels better, his spirits rise, his mind is made up. He digs fussily in the drawers of his desk and says, "I will give him a pocket watch." He finds it. "He is still a

[1] A novel by Gogol.

young man, he needs a pocket watch so he can please his fiancée
. . ." etc. He blows the dust from it, looks at it closely, runs to the
door to prevent his guest from leaving but stops halfway.

'And here we can have what is called a "grand" pause. A man
who a moment ago was burning with a desire to give a present as
quickly as possible, is now horrified at the thought he has almost
committed an unpardonable extravagance, that threatened him
with ruin.

'This is not a sudden thought. It must arise and grow during the
pause. Once he has understood all the implications, he has the task
of hiding the precious object he had almost let slip out of the
house for as long as he can. He cannot rest until he can be sure
that the object is really hidden and keeps changing the hiding
place. The watch is finally stowed in a good place . . . But what
about his benefactor? No problem – "I'll leave it to him in my will
so he can remember me."

'Plyushkin is himself again. He anxiously begins to examine his
belongings. Has his unexpected visitor gone off with something?

'At this point, the curtain falls.

'Each of these bits must be played truthfully, in logical
sequence. They must develop what has gone before and form them
into an unbroken line of action.

'Don't think about character, about what you feel or experience.
You have a series of episodes, all of which are very different in
their feelings. You can't give them all the same mood – meanness,
moroseness, etc. There is also kindness, generosity and joy. All
your actions differ accordingly. The unexpected change from one,
often completely opposite, action to another reveals the miser at
work in search of personal gain. Develop each episode to the full,
turn everything into actions. Create the pattern of your physical
behaviour in each episode and then bring them all together in a
single line of action. That is an infallible way to embody the ideas
Gogol has put into the character.'

'And what should be my line?' I asked.

'You should in every instance adapt to the other actor.
Plyushkin is a difficult case, but you have to get to the very heart
of him. He has to like you. How do you do that? Put yourself in
Plyushkin's place and think about what he needs. Everyone thinks
he is a miser, but you must be amazed by his generosity, his
hospitality, so that you make him trust you. This is what he says
about his neighbour, the captain: "He is a relative," he says, "he

calls me uncle, uncle, and he kisses my hand, but I am as much his uncle as he is my grandfather." You see, he didn't believe the man, although he kissed his hand. So, you have to be very subtle. You must get to the heart of all Plyushkin's worries, understand them, sympathise with him, become Plyushkin for the moment.

'Perhaps it would be a good idea for you to rehearse all the other landowners he has dealings with, not Chichikov, for a while. That would undoubteldly be of value to you.'

The other actor who played Plyushkin was Petker, who came to the Moscow Art Theatre, like me, from the Moscow Theatre of Comedy (formerly the Korsh). This young artist was a gifted character actor, and when it came to finding an understudy for Leonidov, he was chosen. Stanislavski came to know this new actor by working with him.

After some preparatory rehearsals with the co-directors, Telesheva and Sakhnovski, he was called for rehearsals with Stanislavski. He was summoned one or two hours before the rest of us, and I learned what happened in my absence from his own lips.

At the appointed time Petker entered a small courtyard where Stanislavski was sitting at a table under a canvas sunshade. Next to him were Telesheva and Sakhnovski. A little further off were the designer Simov and the Turkish director Miskhin-Bey, who had recently arrived in Moscow for a festival, and was interested in the technique of directing. Stanislavski had given him permission to sit in on rehearsals.

Stanislavski greeted Petker very warmly and introduced him to Simov and Miskhin-Bey.

After a short pause Stanislavski turned to the other directors and asked them how rehearsals were going, what was working and what was not. Having received reassuring answers to all his questions, he asked:

'And what about age? Plyushkin is seventy years old, at least. It's a great problem.'

The other directors tried to reassure him. 'Petker has created a very good character,' they said. 'He's quite used to playing old men.'

'Hm! . . . Hm! . . . I'm very much afraid that was "old man acting". Look at any young man and see how well he plays someone old. He doesn't, and that is of no interest at all for Gogol's character – the embodiment of universal miserliness . . .

Well, let's try. Start anywhere in the scene. Sakhnovski, prompt me. I'll do Chichikov. So, let's begin.'

Within his limitations, Petker tried to portray a decrepit old miser in the standard manner.

Stanislavski gave him his cues and watched him closely then stopped and asked:

'Who are you talking to? Who is sitting opposite you?'

'Stanislavski.'

'Nothing of the sort. I'm a swindler.'

'How's that?'

'You see? Now you're looking at me more closely than when we were playing the scene. Now there's something living. If I were a known swindler, how would you look at me while we were talking? Now, just look at me as though I were a swindler. Try to guess my intentions, define them. Do I have a knife hidden somewhere? Think of somewhere at home where you have hidden your prized possession. Don't do any acting. Just visualise it for yourself. You keep wanting to act. You can't act anything yet, get your thoughts in order.'

Then Stanislavski reached for his pen, which was lying on the table, so as to make notes but in a sudden move Petker grabbed it and put it out of reach.

'Perfect. Now try and guess what I want to do next. Look at me. No, don't act, really look. You're still acting! . . . Let's take a walk round the courtyard. I am your neighbour and this is your property. Tell me in detail how things are with you. What's this barn for?' he asked in all seriousness, pointing to a building.

Petker replied in general terms but Stanislavski wasn't satisfied and kept asking questions about details.

At that moment a cart made a delivery. Stanislavski immediately went to it, on the way asking what was being delivered and why.

Petker explained. Stanislavski listened attentively, but repeated his questions several times and wasn't satisfied until he got a comprehensible answer. So they walked round the courtyard and went on with their game in a very serious tone, then sat at the table and continued their conversation about the property – the mowing, the harvest, the peasants, etc.

While they were talking, I arrived. I saw Stanislavski in serious conversation with Petker. It never occurred to me they were rehearsing and I stopped at some distance waiting for the right moment to say hello.

Stanislavski glanced at me and whispered quietly to Petker: 'Look who's come. Be very careful of him, don't go near, he's a swindler.'

I realised what was happening and joined in the game.

Stanislavski had prepared the ground and suddenly changed from a landowner into a director and began to watch us closely.

I went up to Petker and he quickly jumped up and ran away.

'Hm! . . . Hm! . . . You're acting, Petker. You only need go a few steps away . . . Now, Toporkov, go up to him again. Hm! . . . still "acting". Chichikov will understand at once that you're afraid of him, so you must only do what is necessary to get out of danger.'

Gradually Petker and I began to talk, improvising at first in our own words and then went on to the script. Every time our conversation began to look like acting and stopped being human, Stanislavski interrupted us. Again and again, he brought us back to truth.

'You don't need acting. You just have to listen and work out where your conversation with Chichikov is leading. All I need is for you to concentrate . . . Try to guess why this uninvited guest has arrived. Now, ask him to sit down . . . No, not like that, he could stick a knife in you . . . No, not like that either . . . find a more easy way . . . and less dangerous.'

Step by step, he dug living responses out of the actor and cleared away everything that was histrionic, routine and stagy. He even got rid of Petker's usual 'old man' acting, and a living face appeared, with wary, mistrustful eyes. I responded to him as I should and we both began to sense a bond of mutual interest between us. I began very carefully to state my business. He listened to me, trying to see what it was really about.

We felt good. The tiny audience listened to our conversation and watched its course.

There came the moment when Petker, as Plyushkin, fully appreciated the favour Chichikov wanted to grant him, and after my line, 'Out of respect for you I will take the cost of the purchase on myself', his face lit up. He was silent for a long while and looked at me in amazement. Our audience waited with great interest for what was to follow. Petker's face twitched convulsively. Up to this point Stanislavski had been sitting in silence, trying not to interrupt the scene which was now on the right track. Now he carefully suggested:

'Now you can overact, overact with your face, overact as much as you like. You've won the right to. Screw it up as much as you can, stick your tongue out . . . more . . . more . . . Don't be afraid . . . Yes!'

He gave a happy laugh as he spoke and everyone else laughed, too. With that, he ended the rehearsal.

'That was very good . . . you understand how carefully you have to feel your way into a role, carefully spin fine threads together and not break what you have woven? They will then form a strong rope of their own accord, which will be difficult to break. Go on working, don't force anything, cautiously make your starting point the most simple, living, organic actions. Don't think about the character. The character will emerge as a result of your performing truthful actions in the given circumstances. You have just seen, in this example, how you can build a pathway by going from one small truth to another, testing yourself out, releasing your imagination and so achieve a vivid, expressive character. Go on working in that spirit. Do you understand what you have to do?' he said, turning to the co-directors. 'Come back and show me a little later.'

But we never, in fact, had an opportunity to show the scene to Stanislavski again. He was busy with other things. Once he telephoned me and asked how Petker was doing in his role. We talked for two hours. The enormous interest he had in the role and the new actor was evident. I found it difficult to answer because my position was very delicate. If you reassured him, he stopped believing you and started asking tricky questions to catch you out, like a police inspector, but if you talked about mistakes or what had gone wrong, you were 'selling out' a friend and needlessly upsetting Stanislavski.

I was as evasive as I could be. In reply to a worrying question about the problem of age, I overdid it: 'Oh, don't worry about that . . . Petker is dealing with that problem splendidly . . . it's amazing how he manages to show a very, very old, sick man.'

'Hm! . . . Hm! . . . if he is being ill, that's terrible . . . What does ill mean? Mentally ill? That's of no interest whatsoever. The idea here is that Plyushkin has a mania for hoarding. So will Chichikov when he is old. Plyushkin's joints are stiff, he can't stand up or sit down easily, his sight is poor . . . that's all . . . but for the rest he is perfectly healthy and normal.'

'Let us come and see you, we would like to show you the scene again.'

'I'll try, but you see, there's no time, I have other things . . . I don't know whether I can. But do please call me and tell me what's happening . . . And don't . . . hide things . . . Hm . . . Hm . . . Will you have a candid chat with me . . . Ah?'

'Of course.'

'Goodbye.'

At Korobochka's

What an absolute joy it is when, while you are acting, you manage, even for just a few moments, to move into a dimension where everything becomes genuine, when, on stage, there is a sense of real life in all its delicacy of detail. The actor opposite you is a living person. You see him as real, you guess what he is thinking by the expression on his face and the movements of his eyes. Your thoughts, too, are genuine. You feel free to take the pauses that you need in order to understand a situation. You feel no obligation to the audience, you wage a continuous, subtle and fascinating struggle with the other actor or actors. Today is not like yesterday, and tomorrow will not be like today.

All Stanislavski's thinking was intended to rid an actor of everything that held him down to the level of a routine performer, and to lead him to the threshold of organic, human creativity. He had an infinite number of ways of doing this, based on a subtle understanding of the actor's creative process and great experience in the study of all an actor's ailments, which his method was intended to cure.

The role of Korobochka, the landowner was given to Lilina,[1] one of the founder members of the Moscow Art Theatre, a wonderful actress, who had created a brilliant succession of roles. At the time I am writing about, she was trying out new roles, and Korobochka was one of her first as an old woman. This is the main reason why she had such trouble. She was an actress with a gift for comedy, where she was in her element, and had spent years playing charming young women and girls. Korobochka was one of her first old parts, and she was a little lost when trying to come to terms with an elderly landowner, which was unfamiliar material

[1] Stanislavski's wife. She was about sixty-five at the time.

for her, quite apart from Gogol's style. Her infallible intuition gave her nothing. She studiously blocked off every avenue of escape, there was not an open crack to get through. She applied a working method that was unfamiliar to her – painstaking, destructive analysis, needless reflexion, tight self-control – all of which killed her most valuable qualities – instant intuition, naivety and personal charm. What Stanislavski said about another of our actresses can be applied to her: 'You don't have to understand everything in the scene, only some of it. Being too meticulous is sometimes a scourge for an actor. She starts to complicate things and puts a pile of unnecessary clutter between herself and the other actors.'

Lost in a maze of far-fetched ideas and needless complications, poor Lilina pushed herself to breaking point, labouring to create Gogol's character, and with every rehearsal, step by step, went the opposite way from where she wanted to go. For all his genius as a teacher, when he tried to help her, Stanislavski could not save the situation. Lilina was in a state of shock, she understood nothing, and her work with Stanislavski was like a reproduction of the scene between Chichikov and Korobochka. Stanislavski very wittily compared the scene 'Chichikov at Korobchka's' to repairing a watch. The watchmaker (Chichikov) knows his business, and tries to get the works going, but every time, at the last moment, when he has released the action, for some reason the mainspring noisily unwinds and he has to start all over again. As an experienced craftsman, Chichikov doesn't lose his composure, but once again calmly starts putting the works back in place, he tightens the screws until the cirital moment when the crack is heard and the spring fully unwinds. Chichikov summons up all his patience and starts work again, and goes on working until, finally, losing all patience, in a fit of rage, he throws the watch on the floor with all his might, and it unexpectedly starts to go. The watch and its works are what is inside Korobochka's head, and Chichikov's task is to get inside the works, find out what is wrong and repair whatever it is that prevents her from understanding him. Korobochka sincerely wishes to sell her dead souls, it's to her advantage, but she's afraid of selling too cheaply and losing an exceptional opportunity to get rich. She's afraid of making a blunder. She doesn't try to understand what Chichikov actually says, but what he doesn't say, his 'subtext'. So, she has one continuous task in her scene with Chichikov – not to make a blunder and not sell too cheap. Therefore, she has to try and work out what Chichikov's precise intentions are. Korobochka, of course, is a feeble-minded idiot, as Chichikov calls her. However, you can't just play an idiot. Her useless activity, her concentration on resolving non-existent difficulties will reveal her stupidity much more vividly. The actress needs to pay genuine attention to her partner's actions and behaviour, and that apparently was the one simple thing which, for all her efforts, Lilina could not do, even with Stanislavski's help.

'You see,' Stanislavski once said, 'it's curious that a brilliant actress, who can play the most subtle moments, can't fulfil the most basic task.'

He went back to Lilina again and again, and tried to free her from her chains, which she had forged by using an uncongenial method of work, but it was no good. She had received a shock, she couldn't perform one free, conscious action. Everything she attempted betrayed acute, unnatural tension. Finally, she had to give up the role for a while so as not to delay the opening night, and so she could continue working without committing herself to a fixed deadline. The role was given to Zueva who gave the first performance.

After some time, when *Dead Souls* had been played many times, Stanislavski invited me to Leontievski Lane to rehearse the scene with Lilina. I went with a light heart. The rehearsal was for Lilina, I would merely give her the lines, my role was complete, I'd played it many times, but to see Stanislavski at work from the side was important, instructive and no trouble at all. But things proved otherwise. Quite unexpectedly Stanislavski concentrated fully on me. He paid no attention to Lilina's first few lines while I couldn't even open my mouth before I was stopped by his shouting at me. I was in for a bad time.

'What are you doing?'

'I'm shaking the rain off.'

'In the first place, that's not the way it's done, and second, why do you do it next to the table? It's not very polite to your hostess.'

'But he doesn't see his hostess.'

'I don't believe it. How can he not see her? How can you not see her?'

'That's how we've staged the scene at the theatre, but in this room . . .'

'I'm not interested in staging, but logic. If you arrived all wet,

what would you do here, today in the given circumstances? Awful!
. . . What are you doing?'

   – I . . . want . . .

'I don't believe a word . . . '
We got through the opening of the scene somehow and came to
the dialogue:

   – Tea, little father?
   – I don't mind, little mother.

'Awful! Blah, blah, blah. I don't understand a word! . . .'

   – I don't – mind, lit-tle moth-er.

'Go on . . .'

   – What will you have with your tea, little father. There's some
   fruit cordial in the bottle.
   – I don't mind, little mother, with bread and cordial . . .

'Oh dear, oh dear, oh dear . . . You've forgotten everything . . .
You're just saying words. How will you behave at the table?
You're being treated to tea and cordial. She's being attentive to
you, so you respond in the same manner. I don't see any of that.
So, let's begin . . .'
The more we went on, the more niggling he became towards
me. He paid Lilina no attention at all. She was, I thought, not at
her best.
I was in complete despair. I tried with all my might to get away
from Stanislavski's merciless, mesmerising gaze. Just one final
effort and I will ditch everything, leave the rehearsal come what
may. But suddenly . . . what was this? My words were coming out
warmly, they were alive. I stretched out for the decanter on the
table, poured a glass of cordial, glanced at Korobochka, saw
Lilina's clear, attentive eyes (up till then I had seen them as
though in a haze) and felt a need to communicate with her.

   – What is your name? (I asked.) Excuse me . . . for making
   myself so much at home, it was night when I arrived . . .

My apology sounded sincere. Stanislavski said nothing and, in
fact, I had forgotten him. I was only interested in the old lady
sitting opposite me. Little by little, we struck up a pleasant
conversation. She told me about her life, lamented the failures she

had had, and suddenly everything was of interest. I wanted to work on her, buy all her dead souls for fifteen roubles . . . The old woman, visibly, was dim, I could finish my business in a couple of minutes.

- Sell them to me, little mother.
- How can I sell them?
- Simple . . .
- But they're dead.
- Who said they were living? You pay taxes for them but I will relieve you of all the bother and the payments and I will give you fifteen roubles into the bargain. You understand?
- Truly, little father, I can't get it into my head . . .

I see Lilina's bright eyes. Sometimes they fix greedily on me, sometimes they glide over the money. I wait for their answer. I don't need words, I can see they are full of doubt.

- You see, little mother (I try to explain), it's money, money, and that doesn't grow on trees . . . How much did you sell your honey for? That sin is on your conscience, little mother.

Lilina is living Korobochka's thoughts so truthfully, I can tell her intentions without her lines.

- Fine, but that was honey . . . honey. There's nothing really to sell here, so I'll give you fifteen not twenty roubles for nothing, and not in coin but in banknotes.

I see a glimmer of understanding in Lilina's eyes, the business will go well, but suddenly:

- No, I'm still afraid of making a loss . . .

The spring unwound with a snap. I sat down opposite Lilina and, in silence, began to look at her, trying to work out what was the best approach. To my surprise I heard laughter from the people who were watching. Paying no attention, I once more started to work on Korobochka. But hardly had I fixed my eyes on her and prepared to clinch the business than I almost burst out laughing when I saw Lilina transformed into Gogol's comic old woman, the landowner Korobochka. Her eyes were fixed on me, a little confused but full of curiosity. They expressed such impenetrable stupidity, and they took me, my actions, my thoughts so seriously that I had to make a great effort to get a hold on myself and take the matter as seriously as she did.

The rest of the scene went like clockwork. We asked each other questions, tried to guess each other's thoughts and intentions, trick each other, frighten each other, convince each other, induce pity, we furiously attacked each other, drew back, rested and started the battle all over again. In all our actions, there was logic, purpose, a conviction of the importance of what we were doing and a concentration on each other. We didn't think about the audience. We were not in the least interested in whether we were acting well or not. We were doing what we were doing. I had to make the incomprehensible mechanism in Korobochka's head work at any cost. That was my sole purpose. We didn't do anything special. It was all very simple, with no comedy tricks and yet the little audience, and Stanislavski, fell on the floor laughing. Stanislavski was almost ill. I think, at that moment, we were very near to Gogol. It was the kind of grotesque even Stanislavski could not reject.

'What did we have here?' asked Stanislavski at the end of the rehearsal. 'You were carried away by an upsurge of intuition, and played the scene extremely well. Intuition is the most valuable thing in the arts. Without it they do not exist. You will never be able to play the scene that way again. You may play worse, you may play better but you won't play what you did just now again. Try to repeat it, and it won't work. You can't pin it down permanently. You can only pin down the way that led to that result. I gave you a hard time, Toporkov, so you would find a sense of truth in the simplest physical actions. That is the way to arouse your intuition. I drove you along the path of simple logic, sequence, of genuine, human communication. Once you were aware of the logic of your behaviour, you believed in your actions and the stage was genuinely alive. We control this logic, we can fix it, understand it and it is the path to intuition. Study this path, think of nothing else and the results will follow. I helped Toporkov to take his first steps, then he made his own way, without any help.'

'And Lilina?'

'Lilina simply began to take an interest in our work, the process of gradually bringing Toporkov to life. Once she became interested, she began to pay real attention to him and that means genuine concentration on the object. We cleared away all the obstacles, freed her from her chains, and led her towards living communication with a living person. Each had an effect on the other, they sparked each other off, and you saw the quality of the result.'

It was clear to me why Stanislavski had only concentrated on me and completely ignored Lilina in this rehearsal when, essentially, it had been called for her. This was a particular way to get to a particular actress.

Much later, in a rehearsal for *Tartuffe*, Stanislavski said:

'Many people know the system, but very few can apply it. I, Stanislavski, know the system but I still can't, or rather, I'm still just starting to apply it. If you want to master the system I have developed, you must be born again, and live until you are sixty and start acting all over again.'

This thought which Stanislavski expressed is a final answer to all those who propound the system, whether they accept it or reject it.

The Council

In the play there is a scene called 'The Council Scene': the frightened and daunted officials gather at the Prosecutor's house for a 'council' meeting to discuss the scandalous rumours about Chichikov that are running all over the town. They could have dire consequences. I was not in that scene, except for one line, spoken outside the door, and so had the opportunity to watch all the subtlety of Stanislavski's directing from the wings. This may well be the best scene in the play, its high point. Here the true character of all those involved in Chichikov's weird, incomprehensible scheme with the dead souls was revealed. This comparatively small but vivid scene had been brilliantly put together by the adaptor, Bulgakov. All Gogol's most piquant ideas and situations are concentrated in it. In our preliminary work on the play we had tended to overdo everything and, in this scene, Sakhnovski and Telesheva had gone all out to find the extreme and the grotesque in all its forms. They wanted to out-Gogol Gogol. But no matter how much they tried, no matter how many clever ideas they had, not one of them worked, they merely tired the actors out. What, in Gogol's original, rang out as convincing, truthful and typically mordant, just seemed extremely overdone in performance. Outside, it was supposed to be hard-edged, but inside it was cold, empty and unconvincing. The actors did not believe anything they were doing on stage.

When Stanislavski started work on the council scene, the first thing he did was to call the exaggerated, external methods we had applied into doubt. He indicated their lack of logic.

'Why do you pull such faces when you come into the room?'

'We're terrified. We've been scared by recent events.'

'You can't play terror ... you have to save yourself from danger, but the danger isn't in here, it's out there, where you just came from. You're at home in this room, but you're still looking afraid of something. You have no logic. Instead of relief, you're trying to "act" terror, and what you do is both tasteless and exaggerated as well. Heightened form can only be achieved through the logical sequence of your behaviour. If I don't believe your logic, you'll never convince me of anything, even if you walk on your hands and stick on five noses and eight eyebrows. I saw one very good actor, playing in a light comedy, take off his trousers and hit his mother-in-law with them. It was wonderful and not in the least shocking because the actor was able to convince the audience that his behaviour was logical and that he had no alternative. He prepared us gradually, step by step, for it. So, you want heightened forms? Start first with truth of content, genuine human feelings, the logical sequence of action, and gradually develop it as far as it needs to go.'

As he worked on this scene, Stanislavski took a completely different direction from the one we had taken: there was no exaggeration, no overacting. Every attempt to add something 'extra' was rooted out.

'What are you doing with that handkerchief?'

'Wiping my forehead.'

'Why?'

'He was terrified and his forehead was bathed in sweat, so he wiped it.'

'Nobody wipes his forehead like that. That's ham. You're not wiping your forehead, you're "acting" again. Try to wipe your forehead naturally.'

Everyone in the scene took part in a lengthy exercise. And then, in succession, Stanislavski spent a long time on apparent trifles, simple physical actions of no visible significance, and insisted they be done properly. Having selected this climatic moment in the play, Stanislavski deliberately reduced it to work on the simplest elements of an actor's technique. Never before had he been so meticulous in the application of his method.

The scene was now vivid, it held your interest, it had the right tension. But Stanislavski did much subtle, complex work on it, giving the actors a more organic awareness of the events. One, two, three officials enter. The amount of time Stanislavski spent on each entrance!

'Remember, there's a threat hanging over you . . . You are linked by a common danger . . . Try to look to each other to see who has a way out. Now you're here, you feel easier, you're among friends. Be aware of that, and don't act more than you have to, don't overact. Just come in and realise you are all friends together. Relax your muscles! So! No, not like that. The entrance of each official must be a scene on its own. You've tiptoed the whole way here as if under fire, but as soon as you cross the threshold you are relatively safe. Try to find a solution in the eyes of everyone there while they look for salvation in yours. Just do that, don't add anything more. The through-action for all of you is to find a way out of the situation. Pay close attention to every suggestion. What does that mean? You latch on to anyone who opens his mouth, you look at them and quickly size them up . . . Don't take your eyes off them, you must stick together.'

We did a whole series of 'concentration' exercises. It was a long time before Stanislavski got beyond the first entrance and meeting of the three officials in the room at the Prosecutor's house. He demanded fully organic behaviour and rigorous concentration. He began with simple, physical actions and demanded absolute precision and polish. He made the actors start from comprehensible logic, he did not force anything, didn't overburden them with tasks that were beyond them, but merely cleared the way they were to follow.

Stanislavski helped them master, one by one, the elements of living, human behaviour, and made them concentrate properly on each other. That produced a much more vivid effect that the exaggerated emotions they had used earlier. He didn't tell the actors how to play the scene, didn't demonstrate in any way. He applied his method in all its subtlety and inventiveness. He set each of the actors on the path of logic, of belief in the truth of their actions, rather than let them 'act', and helped them discover their own vital humanity in their roles. Their initiative, their dynamism, gave us the hope that the scene would grow, and heighten. The actors seemed gradually to discover the alarm the officials felt. One could believe that everyone present was under a great strain. There was a feeling of conspiracy. The actors began to believe in themselves, in their actions. Truth was created. It was very watchable, but it still didn't go beyond an exercise. Work continued. Stanislavski painstakingly and carefully put flesh on the bare bones of the scene.

The Police Chief enters. He has come from the inn where Chichikov is staying. Everyone rushes up to him.

'And?'

'He was rinsing his mouth out with milk and figs.'[1]

'Awful!' Stanislavski's voice interrupted him. 'You have just ruined everything we've been doing. I didn't understand a word of what you said.'

'He was rinsing his mouth out with milk and figs.'

'You see what important news you bring: "He's rinsing his mouth out with milk and figs." How do you judge that? As something positive or negative? You see, you haven't made up your mind, but you still start talking. Oh dear, oh dear, oh dear! So! Where have you come from with this news?'

'From the inn.'

'So tell us how you got there, what your plans were, how you spied on him and so on.'

'I . . . went to the inn . . . asked which room Chichikov was in . . . looked through the keyhole and saw him rinsing his mouth.'

'Is that all? Dear heaven, what paucity of imagination! This is a real event! The Police Chief is tracking down a criminal – that's something! He has to work out a plan and make an arrangement with the innkeeper through a go-between, so that he can enter unseen, incognito. You can imagine what an uproar there would be otherwise. You might even disguise yourself. Who knows what might happen! Think it all over thoroughly. To get this valuable information about "rinsing his mouth out with figs" the Police Chief needs great effort, talent, inventiveness and skill. When you bring it, don't undersell it, as you did just now. You're not bringing the things that have happened on stage with you, because you don't know what they are. This is important for everyone. Each person has to know not just what is being performed on stage but what led up to it and what will follow in every detail. If that doesn't happen, you understand, you won't know what it is you are acting. It all hangs together. The role must be like a

[1] Milk sweetened with fig juice. A mouthwash of the period.

continuously running film. Without that, you won't be able to play the scene, which is broken down into fragments. So, try to tell me what the Police Chief did at the inn.'

Stanislavski subjected everyone in the council scene to a thoroughgoing treatment, using one or other of his prescriptions so he could draw organic behaviour out of them. The 'grotesque' or exaggeration were never mentioned. Only logic and truth in the performance of their actions. Slowly the scene in the Prosecutor's room came to life.

The officials are scared witless and run round the room like things possessed, snatching first at one suggestion then another, and rejecting them, frightened by the slightest sound, like the screeching of the parrot. In this panic-stricken mood, they are ready to believe any story about Chichikov's secret activities. If only they could learn the truth, they would be able somehow to ward off disaster.

The most valuable aspect of this scene was the level of seriousness which Stanislavski was able to elicit from the actors. All the humour of the scene was there, which was the reason for the preliminary exercises and all the laborious and painstaking work. The results were striking. What a wonderful base for the later scene, when Nozdriov spins lies. He comes into the room where the terrified officials are. He is happy, a little tipsy, and he is not in the picture. Far from encountering the usual mistrust, he is, on the contrary, egged on by the officials in his lies. They watch his lips, hanging onto his every word. How could he not lie? How deadly serious the actors were, and what a contrast with the first scene ('The Governor's Reception') when everyone shunned him and tried to avoid any kind of contact with him! Now it was all different. Nozdriov talks and everyone listens, they even suggest topics for his lies.

'Hasn't he been a forger?'

'Yes.'

'Wasn't he also a spy?'

'Yes.'

'It's a terrible thought but hasn't it been rumoured in the town that Chichikov is Napoleon?'

'Yes.'

What freedom this is for Nozdriov, how he wallows in the unprecedented attention that is paid to his lies. How easy it was for Moskvin to deliver Gogol's wonderful lines in response to such genuine attention! The genuine seriousness of the attention the officials paid to Nozdriov produced equally intense concentration in the audience as they watched the events on stage. And how wonderfully Stanislavski worked with Moskvin, once playing bits of Nozdriov with him!

It is important for the actor playing Nozdriov not to 'act'. The others act for him. And he doesn't have to be very drunk either. That would be of little interest. Someone really drunk will lie about God knows what. There's nothing special about that. Nozdriov is slightly drunk and blooms in the atmosphere of trust and attention around him. This atmosphere was created by Stanislavski's wonderful skill and mastery.

Ball and Supper at the Governor's

Stanislavski's self-appointed task, when directing this gala scene ('Ball and Supper at the Governor's') was to build up the lead character's through-action still further.

The ball and supper at the Governor's, which takes a whole act in the adaptation, is almost a mime scene. The text is practically non-existent. This could be a golden opportunity for a director to expand and create a vivid picture of a provincial ball, in all its glitter and grandeur. Stanislavski rejected this solution. He staged the whole act very discreetly, so as not to distract attention from the main character, Chichikov, who might get lost in a mass of bright colours. The ball and the supper must be a background for him, highlighting his actions when he is at the peak of his fame, and his fall, which is witnessed by the whole assembly. And how masterfully, how effectively he did it! In this scene, Chichikov, who only has four or five lines throughout, was the centre of the audience's attention the whole time. When the curtain rises, the audience sees a vast room in the Governor's house and hears music. The older guests, ladies and gentlemen, are seated downstage on chairs and sofas, while young people are dancing upstage. The ball is not especially lively or cheerful, it has not yet reached its height, but now we see a lot of whispering and, here and there, groups of guests begin to get excited. Evidently some sort of news is spreading. Finally, from different parts of the room we hear the excited cry, 'Chichikov, Chichikov!'

Gradually, everyone starts looking towards the door though

which, to everyone's delight, the glorious Chichikov emerges, resplendent in his evening dress and gloves. He passes from one group to another, and is warmly greeted everywhere, etc., etc. Every step he takes adds to the impact of his arrival. All the ladies try surreptitiously to pin a ribbon on his coat.[1] When he ends his conversation with the Governor's daughter and goes to table, his coat is covered with glittering favours. In the vast expanse of the ballroom, or at table, or amid a horde of guests, Chichikov is never for one moment out of the audience's eye, despite the fact that, essentially, he does nothing. Others 'do' it for him. Chichikov is always in the foreground and so the ball and the supper advance the plot, and keep the audience's attention on him.

Our work on the beginning of this act was rather out of the ordinary. Stanislavski started with the overall rhythm of the guests' behaviour. He was like a conductor. He asked the actors, sitting at the table, to vary their behaviour in highly different rhythms. A few rhythmic patterns were established, from the neutral, that is static, to the extremely active. There were twenty people sitting at the table, talking quietly. Half of them were speaking, half of them were listening. The voices were low and silky. That was rhythm no. 1. Rhythm no. 2 was almost identical but the voices were a little louder. For rhythm no. 3, the voices were still louder and the tempo very rapid, while those who were supposed to be listening already tended to interrupt the speakers. For rhythm no. 4, the voices were still louder, the tempo was not only tighter, but it was more ragged, the listeners had stopped listening and merely tried to interrupt the speakers. With rhythm no. 5, everyone is talking at once, not listening, and in very loud voices. Their speech had a bouncing, syncopated rhythm. Rhythm no. 6: extremely loud sounds, extreme syncopation, nobody is listening, all they want is to be heard, etc., etc. The whole thing was like a musical exercise rather than the rehearsal of a play. It was remarkable, fascinating. No one could remain indifferent. They were all caught up, like it or not, in the same rhythm, and everyone gave in to its magic and justified it. I already had some ideas about rhythm but I had never before been aware it could be so clear and defined. This was something new for me. I was amazed how what seemed like purely mechanical exercises could result in such a living, organic, subtle, colourful and expressive

[1] To show he will dance with her.

sequence of human behaviour. But it would be a mistake to think that such results are easily achieved, or that all you have to do is establish a range of different rhythms and start to move. Later, I saw expressive moments of tension on stage achieved by purely external rhythm. But it never produced a lasting impression if it remained merely external. The ability to lead an actor to an inwardly justified rhythm, to create genuine tension and living, organic dynamism, is one of the most difficult aspects of directing technique and so is often replaced by stage conventions.

As he continued working further on the Governor's ball, Stanislavski increasingly refined the details, giving each one its proper place in the scene. He devoted a great deal of time and trouble to perfecting the purely external features of the behaviour of the guests at the ball: how the servants should bring in the salvers and serve the food to the guests, how the guests in their turn should offer the food to the ladies, how the men should ask the ladies to dance, or offer them a chair, take them in to supper, how the guests were to eat, drink, clink glasses, hold their knives and forks, etc., etc. Sometimes he would spend hours on one of these apparent trifles, demanding that the actors should perform these actions exactly, deftly, appropriately. He didn't relax until the manners of the cast were perfect, in period and right for the character they were playing. He trained the actors first one way, then another, united them all in a common task, and finally created a beautiful, subtle stage picture within which the actors were able to do splendid improvisations, which lost nothing of their clarity and brilliance over the years.

In his talk to the cast prior to the opening night of *Dead Souls*, Stanislavski said:

'I'm allowing the play to be put on, although it's not really ready . . . It's still not Gogol, but I can see in what you are doing the living seeds of what in the future *will* be Gogol. Follow that path and you will find Gogol. But it won't be tomorrow.'

Privately, he said to me:

'You have only just recovered from your illness, you have learned to walk and to a certain extent deal with actions. The living line of actions is still weak, you must make it stronger. In five or six years, you'll be able to play Chichikov and in twenty you'll understand what Gogol means.'

The reviewers were severely critical of us. Of course, on the first night we didn't present the immortal novel as well as it deserved. But then who could? The 'art' critics contrasted our production to the work of another theatre, of formalist tendency, one of those I spoke of earlier, and maintained that it would be able to find a brilliant solution to this difficult problem, if it used its whole battery of techniques.

History has shown how mistaken this view was. Formalist theatres have long since gone out of existence.[1] But *Dead Souls*, in which the seeds of genuine, meaningful art had been planted, continued, as Stanislavski had predicted, to grow and continued to run for fifty years and enjoyed constant success with Soviet audiences. And in particularly successful performances, in one or two scenes, the actors achieve an intensity in which the real Gogol can be felt.

Stanislavski's concern for the actor extended beyond the confines of the theatre. He understood the importance of the influence of everything on an actor's being and his creative powers and so kept a close watch on all outside factors that would have a good or bad influence on him. He was constantly concerned with anything that might be of help to an actor in difficult moments and never missed an opportunity to get him out of trouble. This applied not only to leading but more modest actors, especially the young.

During the time that I managed the company, I talked to Stanislavski about our actors. This was often on the telephone. He knew who each actor was, and how, and to what extent, he could be useful to the theatre, and tried to give me his opinions.

'To create art in the highest sense, you need an enormous range of mood and colour. Some of them will only rarely be used, but they need to be available to us. It is the same with the Art Theatre. Our company is our artist's palette, each actor is valuable, like a unique colour. We have to care for him, no matter how humble his position is. It would be hard for us to find a replacement. He has grown up with us and is part of our ethos.

'Part of your responsibility is to protect our most valuable asset, the actor, without whom the theatre cannot exist. This concern must extend not only to large matters but to all the tiny details of an actor's life. Do you realise what a heavy burden you bear?'

---

[1] Toporkov is referring, among other things, to Meyerhold's theatre which was brutally closed in 1936. Meyerhold was executed in 1940.

Tartuffe

Preliminary Discussion and the Beginning of Work

Stanislavski's final, and incomplete, project at the Moscow Art Theatre was Molière's *Tartuffe*. He started work with a small group of actors not long before his death, with a strictly educational end in view. So it would be true to say it was not a question of rehearsing a play, as such, but of improving the technique of the actors involved.

One of Stanislavski's lifelong concerns, as we know, was to discover new, improved methods that would enable an actor to work on himself and on a role. For Stanislavski, progress, even if it were only one step, was the progress of the actors who were cast in the play.

He categorically rejected production plans, however daring they might be, that were not warranted by the actors' technical skills, that were not securely lived by them. Better something more modest, simpler, within the actors' capabilities than a fruitless attempt to scale the heights with unsuitable means. A production plan that is not made flesh and blood by acting is still just a plan, not a performance. We may appreciate the director's powers of imagination, but this kind of a production can never touch an audience's heart, and so, in consequence, is of no value.

Stanislavski tried to find theatrical images that would give form and substance to Molière's immortal work using a new, improved, more effective acting technique.

He considered that learning to play the classics was an urgent task for the Soviet stage. But, being a great artist, the traditional cliché-ridden style of acting *Tartuffe* could not satisfy his restless, endlessly creative nature.

The unsatisfactory state of contemporary acting distressed him more and more, and he worried about the future of the Moscow Art Theatre itself. Stanislavski used every meeting with actors and directors to propound his ideas. All his rehearsals inevitably turned into experiments on the nature of the actor's creative process. All his efforts were directed to making sure that not only actors understood and mastered his method, but directors too. To understand, in his sense, meant being able to make it work and to be able to make it work, a director had to be able to get inside an actor's skin. It was thus that the idea of a production cast entirely with directors came into being. He put it into practice. I was a witness to the first rehearsal of this new, directors' production. Ten directors, including Sakhnovski, Telesheva, Gorchakov, gathered in the rehearsal room at Leontievski Lane. There were also observers, including the theatre's business manager Egorov, Stanislavski's secretary Tamantseva, and one or two actors and actresses.

The group gathered in the large room and waited eagerly for Stanislavski to come in. This was, if I am not mistaken, in the spring of 1938, some months before his death. He was not feeling well, his strength was failing, he had just recovered from the flu and there were complications with his legs. Everyone was staring intently at the door through which Stanislavski was due to appear. It was quite late in the day and the room was half dark. A strange group emerged into this semi-darkness, first a nurse in a white uniform, then Stanislavski's tall, stooping figure with his snow-white hair. He was supported under his arms. Moving his legs with difficulty, he went to the table, greeted everyone with a bow and started work.

'So, what were you thinking of doing?' he asked the directors after some conversation on general matters.

'Well, we would rather like to work on Gogol's *Marriage*.'

'*Marriage*? Oh, oh, oh. Why have you chosen such a difficult play? Well ... never mind ... Please ...'

I once read an unfinished and unpublished novel by a very talented Soviet dramatist, now dead. In one chapter, a young writer talks about the troubles he had with his first play in the theatre. (He means the Moscow Art Theatre.)[1] There was a satirical portrait of a director in which it was not difficult to recognise Stanislavski. In the chapter I refer to, there is a description of a moment when a scene is shown to the main director – i.e., Stanislavski – a love scene in which the young author liked the acting very much. He is amazed when the director, having watched it through, declares his dislike of this beautiful scene. He said, more or less: 'Awful! ... This is a love

---

[1] The reference is to Bulgakov and his novel translated into English by Michael Glenny as *Black Snow*. Bulgakov died in 1940. The novel was first published in the Soviet Union in 1965.

scene! But you don't love the lady at all. Do you know what love is? It means she is everything. Understand? I sit down for her, I walk for her. Whatever I do, it is for her. Understand?'

Then suddenly:

'Props!!'

The terrified propsmen run in.

'Bring a bicycle.'

This unexpected request completely dumbfounds the inexperienced dramatist and the two lovers. When the bicycle has been brought 'Stanislavski' suggests to the actor, who is white as a sheet, that he should circle his beloved on it.

'But you must do it for her, understand? Only for her.'

'But I don't know . . . how to ride a bicycle . . . I just don't.'

'But you *must*, for her. So! Please . . .'

The author of the novel obviously thought that he had described this rehearsal cleverly and made good fun of Stanislavski's directing. However, one or two exaggerations apart, which give the incident its humour, the method the author described was typical of Stanislavski. We all knew it well, and it didn't produce the same reactions in us as it did in him.

Something similar to what is described in the novel occurred during the directors' production. Stanislavski suggested to the prospective cast of *Marriage* that they do a simple exercise.

'Please . . . Each of you write a letter. Do it with imaginary objects, but in great detail: how you pick up the pen, how you move the ink bottle, open it, check how much is left, take a sheet of paper, etc., etc. The more detail the better. Don't rush it, get involved in what you are doing, and only do it for yourself, it's not a demonstration . . .'

Stanislavski observed the exercise he had given very closely and made not only the cast but everyone in the room do it. He was critical of details, he made us do the same thing several times over, and, for some reason, mostly addressed his remarks to Egorov, who was there simply out of curiosity.

How the work on Gogol's play, that had started with exercises on simple physical actions quite separate from the play, would have progressed, what the next phase would have been, we can't say. It was the one and only rehearsal. Stanislavski's state of health and other reasons prevented him from continuing his work, which, if you bear in mind the specific tasks he had set himself, would undoubtedly have included new, experimental methods. This work with a group of directors was an incidental part of the radical work Stanislavski had been doing for some time with a group of actors on Molière's *Tartuffe* with Kedrov as their director.[1]

Stanislavski had asked for a selected group of actors – subsequently cast in *Tartuffe* – to be freed from their normal duties at the theatre, with the exception of those who were involved in the current repertoire. He wanted to be sure that he had an opportunity for more productive work, and scope to implement his ideas.

I think that one of the reasons for choosing this play was its small cast, and the theatre could release a small group of actors from their obligations without harm to itself, and hand them over completely to Stanislavski.

A second reason was Stanislavski's wish to give a practical demonstration that his method was universal and not solely applicable to the normal Moscow Art Theatre repertoire (Chekhov), as was generally thought. Besides which, Stanislavski obviously liked the play. He had, as we know, once started work on a production but for some reason never finished it.

The group included Kedrov (director, head of the company and Tartuffe), Knipper and Bogoyavlenskaya (sharing Mme Pernelle), Koreniova (Elmire), Geirot (Cléante), Bedina (Dorine), Bordukov (Damis), Mikheyeva (Marianne), Kislyakov (Valère) and myself as Orgon.

A few changes were made to the cast as work progressed. For certain reasons, Knipper was unable to take an active part in our work and the role of Mme Pernelle went to Bogoyavlenskaya. Only subsequently, after *Tartuffe* had been played many times at the Moscow Art Theatre was Knipper brought into the show, and gave several performances. Bordukov left the group and was replaced by Komissarov. But that happened much later, after Stanislavski's death, when the work of putting the final production together was entirely in Kedrov's hands. Kedrov cast the following actors in minor roles: Voinova (Mme Pernelle's maid), Kurochkin (Loyale) and Kirilin (an officer).

Bogoyavlenskaya and I, as well as acting, also did some directing. Bogoyavlenskaya worked on the scenes with young people, and I supervised the scenes in which Kedrov appeared as an actor.

In his first talk, Stanislavski tried to discuss fully with each of us

[1] Work had begun a year earlier in April 1937.

the nature of our work and our relationships with each other. He wanted us to be open and honest.

'If all you want is to play a new role with a slightly more up-to-date technique, then I am going to disappoint you in advance. I have no intention of putting on a performance, I am no longer interested in theatrical glory. For me to put on one production more or one production less has no meaning for me. What is important for me is to communicate my store of knowledge to you. I want to teach you not how to play one part but every part. Think about that. An actor must work on himself the whole time, improve his skills. He must strive to achieve mastery as quickly as possible, and over all roles, not just the one he is presently studying.

'I ask you to tell me honestly: do you want to learn? Just be sincere. There is no place here for deceit. You are mature people, each of you is a well-known actor, each of you has the right to consider himself a polished professional, you can spend the rest of your lives in the theatre. You may find the prospect of playing two or three brilliant roles more attractive than long, onerous study. I understand that completely. Have the courage to recognise it. I have more respect for honesty than for sham agreement . . . But I must say to you in all honesty, without such study you will be in a blind alley.

'The art we practice in the Art Theatre is such that it demands constantly to be renewed, constant work on oneself. It is based on the reproduction and communication of life as we really live it, it does not tolerate fossilised forms and traditions, however beautiful they may be. It is alive, and, like everything living, in a constant state of flux. What was good yesterday will not do today. Tomorrow's performance is not the same as today's. This kind of acting demands a special technique, not a technique based on the study of existing methods, but the technique of mastering the laws of human creativity, of being able to influence and control that creativity, the capacity to reveal one's creative capabilities, one's intuition in every show. This is an artistic technique, or, as we call it, psychotechnique. This technique and its results must form the foundation of our theatre and set it apart from all others. It is the art of beauty. But, I repeat, it demands constant, regular work on oneself. Otherwise very quickly, and sooner than you think, it will decline, turn to nothing and our theatre will sink below the level of the usual hack theatres. Definitely lower, because those theatres at least have solidly learned, standard techniques, an established tradition handed down from generation to generation. All this maintains them at a certain level, with a certain quality. Our kind of theatre is fragile and if those who create it don't take constant care of it, don't keep moving it forward, do not develop and perfect it, it will soon die.

'Mastering this technique should be the concern of our whole theatre, all the actors and directors. Our art is an ensemble art. Brilliant individual actors in a show are not enough. We have to think of a performance as a harmonious union of all the elements into a single artistic creation.

'As I depart this life, I want to pass the fundamentals of this technique on to you. They cannot be conveyed by words or writing. They must be studied practically. If we achieve good results and you understand this technique you will be able to spread it and develop it further.

'I'll give you a short cut. Basically, the "system" has five to ten rules which will enable you to find the right path in all your roles all your life.

'Remember, every good, self-demanding actor must at certain intervals (four or five years), go back to school. He also has to place his voice – it changes with time – and clean away the dirt, the bad habits he has acquired, like displays of charm, conceit, etc., etc. He must widen his culture and his learning and after five or six years, go back to school for six months or more.

'Do you understand the nature of the task that lies before you? I say again, don't think about a show of any kind, only about study and then more study. If you agree to that, let's start; if not, let's part without any kind of rancour. You'll go to the theatre and get on with your work and I'll form another group and do what I consider to be my duty.'

Work then began. Kedrov was initially in charge under Stanislavski's supervision. It had a very special character. But I'll come to that later.

As everyone knows, for Stanislavski the theatre's future lay in developing and consolidating the realism in which it had its origins. Only conscious realism which truthfully reflects 'the life of the human spirit' is the proper means to touch and educate an audience. Stanislavski found vivid, genuinely organic ways of giving physical form to his radically realistic ideas. For that, he had to lead the actor back to life itself, and clear away the battery of theatrical tricks and clichés which obscured his real human self from the audience.

'When you are rehearsing,' Stanislavski said, 'first, you must start with yourself and who you are; second, you must obey the laws of creativity; third, you must bow to another person's logic, that is to the character as a human being. I can't play any role if I have not thoroughly cleaned the Augean stables of my mind of all its old clichés.'

Stanislavski was searching for a superior form of realistic acting, a further development of the traditions of Russian theatre, one that was much improved, forward-looking and persuasive.

Once he has accepted someone else's logic and made it flesh and blood on stage, an actor's behaviour becomes genuine but at the same time he lives his own feelings; he smells, listens, sees with all the refinement of his own organs and nerves, his actions are genuine, he doesn't playact or represent them.

'Real acting begins,' said Stanislavski, 'when there is no character as yet, but an "I" in the hypothetical circumstances. If that is not the case, you lose contact with yourself, you see the role from the outside, you copy it. When you use the system properly, you may act well, you may act badly, but you won't "act" well, which is the case, say, with Coquelin.[1]

' "Acting" well is a very difficult art. It requires a great deal of time, effort, patience and precision, but it is something which we cannot do and, indeed, do not like doing. And that is all to our good, since Coquelin only makes an impression on you while he is acting, whereas Ermolova?[2] becomes part of your life, your soul.'

Stanislavski inspired his actors and gave them the ability to experience dramatic events afresh, first-hand each time.

'My method is to get involved with the feelings I have today. Here, today, now, I will say, punish Chichikov, I will arrest him, etc. You have been complimented on a certain moment in a role, on a gesture, a line-reading. Don't get too fond of them, don't hang on to them, replace them with something better and avoid their becoming clichés. Take a sponge and wipe them out.'

[1] Constant Coquelin (1841–1909), celebrated French actor, author of *The Art of the Actor*, in which he advocated a purely technical, external approach to the creation of character.

[2] Maria Nikolayeva Ermolova (1823–1928), leading actress at the Maly Theatre, greatly admired by Stanislavski whose work she enthusiastically supported.

It can't be said that Stanislavski brought anything completely new to his final work with us, or anything contrary to his previous teachings about the system, as will be evident from my description of the rehearsals for *Tartuffe*. But now Stanislavski's method was richer, more practical, and that was expressed in the definition, the 'Method of Physical Action'.

We know that throughout his career Stanislavski investigated different key points in his system – rhythm, ideas, tasks, etc. By now his system was entirely based on physical action and he tried to eliminate anything that prevented actors understanding that clearly. When anyone reminded him of his earlier methods, he said that he didn't understand what they were talking about. Once someone asked: 'What is the mood in this scene?'

Stanislavski gave a look of surprise and asked: ' "Mood". And what's that? I've never heard of it.'

That wasn't true. It was an expression he himself had used. However, in the present case, it merely stood in the way, preventing him from pointing us in the right direction. He was very wary of ever looking back, lest it stop him getting where he wanted to go. When one of the actresses told him that she had kept detailed notes of all his rehearsals she'd had with him over a number of years and didn't know what to do with this treasure trove, Stanislavski replied: 'Burn them.'

The most vital and convincing feature of our kind of acting is its sincerity. What is said and done sincerely never raises doubts. Sincere laughter is catching, false, pretended laughter is offensive. Real tears will always touch you, but you will never believe acted grief and false tears. Sincerity is what gives human beings their appeal and charm. An actor who can be sincere on stage cannot but have both. That is why you cannot separate an actor's appeal from his sincerity. Actors who have sincerity in certain roles have appeal, but in others, where they haven't, they are unbearable. We know many actors who have appeal and charm in life, they have physical beauty, fine voices, but no talent for the theatre. Their appeal disappears as soon as they walk on stage.

To have appeal on stage is real theatrical talent.

What is the one quality all our great actors have in common? The sincerity of their behaviour on stage. Why was Varlamov great?[1] What was the secret of his inimitable humour? His pot

---

[1] Konstantin Aleksandrovich Varlamov (1848–1915), a great comic actor at the Alesandrinski Theatre in St Petersburg.

belly, his thick legs, his grotesque shape, his voice? Not at all. There were other actors whose external appearance was just as good as his. Yet Varlamov was unique in the history of the theatre. Varlamov was Varlamov because his talent was unsurpassable, and the quality of his talent lay principally in his capacity to surrender totally to his theatrical imagination and behave in a human fashion on stage. Strelskaya had the same quality.[1] When these two great artists met on stage they created a miracle. They removed the barrier between the stage and life. Often playing in the emptiest, most stupid comedies and sketches, they conquered their audience by the sincerity and truth of their performances. These actors were endowed with this capacity, this theatrical talent, in such abundance that although Varlamov never did any work to develop himself in his entire life, he made his way as a great actor. Had he mastered the other skills that every actor needs, he would undoubtedly have been even greater. Davydov said, 'Give me Varlamov's talent and I will conquer the world.' Yet how priceless what Varlamov had must have been, if it alone could lead him to such great fame.

Stanislavski required actors to have a sense of truth, the ability to give themselves unreservedly to the events in the play easily and sincerely, continuously to follow the logic of their actions, and sincerely to believe in the logic of other people's actions. That's what he wanted from us, the cast of *Tartuffe*. Varlamov could do this intuitively, but it can be achieved to a certain degree by constant hard work. That was Stanislavski's view.

The question as to how to work towards this goal is a complex one. Stanislavski invited us to study it.

He warned us many times against a coldly rational approach to creative work. He required action not talk.

'When an actor is afraid to demonstrate his will, when he has no desire to create, he starts talking. He is like a horse, pawing the ground because it hasn't the strength to move the cart. If you want to act boldly, it's no good pawing the ground, you have to create an overwhelming desire for action. I really want to do something, so I do it boldly. Action comes from the will, from intuition, reasoning comes from the brain, the head. My system only exists to open up an actor's natural power to create. It exists for moments when nothing seems to work.'

[1] Varvara Vasilyevna Strelskaya (1838–1915), a leading actress at the Aleksandrinski Theatre.

Since he considered nature and her workings to be the decisive force in an actor's creative work, Stanislavski created a system for reaching her. He never overlooked the elements of physical behaviour in creating a character. Even when we were working on *The Embezzlers*, I remember how often he drew our attention to the importance of control, clarity and polish even in the most insignificant physical action. It was the same to a greater extent with *Dead Souls*. I have described that earlier. In the last period of his career, in his work on *Tartuffe*, Stanislavski considered this element as supremely important.

One must not think, however, that he thought of physical action and other directorial techniques as ends in themselves, as has often been the case with some of his less talented followers. Every technical device Stanislavski used as a director was only secondary to achieving his principal object – *the fullest possible physical presentation of the concept of a character*. And the choice of physical action and the hypothetical circumstances, etc., were always a means to an end.

It would equally be mistaken to see physical action as no more than expressive movement representing action. No, it is genuine, properly goal-directed, justified action, which, at the moment it is being performed, becomes psychophysical.

When he was working with us, Stanislavski invariably prefaced his remarks with the words:

'So, what sequence of physical action do we have here?'

That meant that the scene had to be translated into the language of physical action, and the simpler the action, the better. For example, the crucial scene between Tartuffe and Elmire, with its alternating long speeches, was reduced to the simplest physical actions. With barely perceptible signs of encouragement, Elmire managed to get Tartuffe to make a false move, and fall into a trap.

'How will you do this? I don't need the dialogue for the moment. Work out a pattern of actions, how you will lure Tartuffe into your net, how you will deal with his feeble advances. And you,' he said to Kedrov, who was playing Tartuffe, 'in your turn, decide, here, now, today what behaviour would be appropriate towards Elmire, who is mistress of the house, and a woman of rank.

'Or, let us take another scene where Orgon is looking for Marianne so he can force her to sign a marriage contract, while Elmire, Cléante and Dorine oppose it. What sort of physical action is there in this scene?

'Don't talk to me about feeling, you cannot set feeling. You can only recall and set physical action. In this particular case we can define the physical action with the verb "to hide". You must hide Marianne from her cruel father. That's what you have to do. So, how? If you use the usual actors' clichés, you will hide her by putting out your hands behind your back and looking anxious, etc., but if you are creative, I don't know how you will do it. But the main thing is "to hide" her.'

He absolutely forbade us to learn the lines. That was an absolute condition of our work and if, suddenly, one of us began to speak Molière's words he immediately stopped the rehearsal. He considered it a kind of impotence in an actor, if he clung to the script, the words, the author's exact words. He considered it a great achievement if an actor could demonstrate the pattern of physical actions in a scene with the minimum of words. Words were to play only an ancillary role.

He absolutely forbade us to use the methods of work that were usual in other theatres. There was no place in our rehearsals for learning the lines by heart or setting the moves. The script was used exclusively to define what the sequence of physical actions was.

Stanislavski told us repeatedly:

'No script, no moves, just know what your scene is about, act out the pattern of physical actions and the role is thirty-five per cent yours already. First, you have to establish the logical sequence of your actions. That's how you prepare.

'Before a painter can move on to the more subtle, complex psychological elements in his picture, he must sketch his ideas on to the canvas and make his subjects "sit", "stand" or "lie down" in such a way we can believe they are actually "sitting", "standing" or "lying down". That is the layout of the picture he will paint. No matter what subtleties he includes in it, if the pose breaks the laws of nature, if there is no truth in it, if the person he has represented as sitting is not really "sitting", no other subtleties will make it successful.

'The sequence of physical actions has the same importance in the art of acting. The actor, like the painter, must make his subject "sit", "stand" or "lie down". But we have a complicating factor: we are both artist and subject and we need to find not a static pose but a living, active person in a wide variety of circumstances. And the actor must not think of anything else until he can create and sketch in this pattern, and can believe in the truth of his physical behaviour in that pattern.'

In the final phase of his experiments, Stanislavski attached the highest significance to the work of creating the pattern of physical actions in a role.

'When we are working on a role,' he said, 'we must first make the sequence of physical actions firmer and stronger. It is even useful to write them down. Second, we must discover their nature. Third, we must be audacious, not think, *do*. Once you start to do something, you will feel the need to justify it.'

If he works along these lines, an actor can genuinely get closer to the kind of acting which Stanislavski called the art of experiencing, as opposed to the art of representation. Genuine, human behaviour, sincerity of experiencing, that is to say, those qualities which are the most truly persuasive in the theatre, which hook an audience and influence their hearts and minds, are the qualities and the art that are personal to great artists and are an example to us.

'You can't master a role right away. There is always something in it you don't understand clearly, something that resists you. So start with what is clearest, most accessible, that is easy to set. Try to discover the truth of the simplest physical actions which are obvious to you. The truth of physical actions will lead you to belief and then to the "I am being" and finally to a flood of creative action. I'm opening the gates to artistic creation for you.'

The method of physical action enables the actor who follows it to achieve belief and a deeper level of experience and feeling. It provides a shorter way to creating a character. At the same time, it is a method of preserving and developing a character that has been created.

'If the sequence of physical actions follows your own personal circumstances in life, if it bears your personal imprint, then there is nothing to worry about if your feelings dry up. Go back to the physical actions and they will restore your lost feelings.'

But physical actions not only point the actor in the right direction when creating a character, they are his best means of expression. And so it was no accident that Stanislavski defined the actor as a master of physical actions. Nothing so clearly and so persuasively conveys a person's mental state than his physical behaviour, that is, a whole series of physical actions. It was not for nothing that great actors often had recourse to them. When we remember the individual theatrical successes Ermolova, Savina, Davydov and Dalmatov had, then in most cases we say: 'Do you remember when they said this or that to her, and how nervously she removed her gloves and threw them on the sofa and went to the table!'

Or:

'Do you remember when her husband wanted to put his cigar butt in the ashtray, and her lover's cigar was already in it, and how she quickly changed it for another?'

'Do you remember how Duse acted with the mirror in the last act of *La Dame aux Camélias*?'

Countless examples could be invoked. Davydov, who was a master of the word, a real virtuoso, nonetheless always crowned the climax of each of his roles with a 'grand' pause, in which with just a few words, or even without any at all, he expressed his character's secret feeling with the utmost clarity through a series of subtly conceived, riveting physical actions and it was only at that precise moment that his real nature was revealed to the audience.

'The workings of our five senses can be broken down into the tiniest physical actions, so write them down and use them as a quick reminder,' Stanislavski said at one rehearsal.

Since he considered physical actions as the prime element in theatrical expression, Stanislavski was always extremely demanding with his actors when they were using them. He always demanded clarity and skill in their execution. He tried to achieve, if we may so express it, good 'diction' in physical actions. He, therefore, recommended that we turn our attention to exercises with imaginary objects, which should be part of an actor's daily 'clean-up'. Exercises with imaginary objects develop concentration, an essential quality in acting. Each time he repeats these exercises, an actor makes them more and more complicated, he divides them into very small sections and so develops the 'diction' of physical actions.

Signing a piece of paper may seem like a single action, but for the actor who is a true artist, it may be one hundred and one actions, according to the circumstances. The act of signing a piece of paper may have no meaning in itself, and superfluous details in such a simple action may irritate. But, on other occasions, it can be the most significant moment in a role and then he will need a hundred and one or more nuances to perform this basically simple action.

I repeat, in the last work he did with actors, Stanislavski placed the greatest importance on the method which he defined as the method of physical actions. 'Nobody really knows this technique which I have developed. But you must work towards it,' he said in rehearsal.

Stanislavski had undertaken his work on *Tartuffe* purely for teaching purposes, and it was accordingly conducted with great rigour and purity of method. No concessions were made to the usual, traditional rehearsal procedures. It would have been difficult to apply them given the very special conditions Stanislavski and Kedrov imposed on us each time. The first phase in rehearsals, which one might call reconnoitring, consisted of getting to know individual scenes and the play as a whole. Kedrov, who took the rehearsals, tried to make every actor give a clear, straight account of the content, or rather, the subject of the play. They had to give just the bare storyline. No unnecessary elaboration was admitted. We only had to answer the question: what is happening, what is going on? The simple, unadorned account of the play should be like one a ten-year-old boy would give, if he had seen the play. As a preliminary step we were recommended to write out the events of the play.

'A certain scoundrel wormed his way into the household of a rich bourgeois, Orgon, under a guise of piety, etc., etc.'

The nature of the account varied according to the questions the director put and the personality of the narrator. But it was always directed towards defining active physical tasks and contained a creative seed within it. The narrator was considered adequate if he found a clear, precise verb to indicate a phase in the developing struggle in Orgon's house. The purpose of narrating the storyline was to establish the through-action and the counter-action. Then it was easy to distinguish the opposing forces on each side and ask all of them:

'If the battle develops in such and such a way, where do you stand in it? What is your position? What is the logic of your behaviour?'

Then came a highly complex, highly difficult, crucial moment in rehearsal, which demanded a great deal of thought and imagination from the actor and a capacity to analyse the material still further. This was the first attempt towards a rough outline of the character, the logic of its behaviour, the logic of the struggle.

An account of his adventures, his successes and failures had to be given not as an outside observer, but as himself, as someone deeply involved in the course of events. In other words, as he speaks, he should live through these events, he should want to engage his listeners in the way they unfold. As well as the oral account, we attempted a written narrative. The literary quality of these narratives was important, because in our attempt to make our writing more exact, we were obliged to probe even deeper in our analysis of the events it described. It was not important for the actor to achieve particularly good results, it was the attempt that was important (generally in our work failure is useful. Success can come much later when an actor least expects it).

You cannot get a totally clear understanding of the character you will play while working at the table. This is only a preliminary exploration, somewhere to start from, something that will undergo all kinds of changes during rehearsal. It is still intellectual work, but I fully appreciated its enormous significance at the end of our work on *Tartuffe* and during the rest of my career. For many this may appear somewhat naive: 'So, what is all this? Of course, first of all I must know what the play is about, decide how the role develops and then rehearse. What's new about that?'

What was new was the nature of the work, its thoroughness. We devoted more time to this 'reconnoitring' than was usual. And it was not a waste. Every session produced fresh results. We had never before seen actors being prepared in this way for later phases in their work. Each of us knew the story of the Orgon family down to the smallest detail. We even started to believe it was a real event, and we felt an overwhelming desire to try to bring it to life on stage. In this way we became committed to this particular method where the director takes the actors through the 'reconnoitring' part of the work.

It involved a great deal of perspicacity and persistence on his part, a capacity to capture and arouse the actors' imagination, so they could evaluate and select events. This provided them with active material that would lead to a full, clear, detailed understanding of the character they were playing, and also to a deeper analysis of the writer's ideas.

The work that followed was notable for one thing, for restraining the actors' natural impulse to rush after quick results. We already knew the play, the dynamic line of the people in it, and characters were beginning to emerge.

'Let's start rehearsing now, even if it's only a tiny scene.'

We felt ready for it, but no, we were stopped again. This time, true, we weren't working at the table, but, as before, the style of working was still unusual for us. We didn't have a particular room or acting space to rehearse in, but two floors of the dressing-room area. They were supposed to represent the two storeys of Orgon's house, a rich bourgeois home with a large number of rooms. The actors were asked to get to know the layout of the house and allocate the rooms among the family. This had to be done in a serious and businesslike fashion. The rooms were not to be allocated with the performance of a dramatic episode in mind, but in response to a genuine, real-life question of how to divide up a house with twenty rooms, each of different dimensions, among a family of ten, all different in age, position and character. We had to decide where the dining room, the bedrooms, the servants' quarters were. Everything had to be comfortably and appropriately divided. We were asked to defend our own interests vigorously, with no compromise. However, all our quarrels had to be conducted in accordance with the existing family relationships. That was very absorbing. There were long discussions, the entire family walked the corridors, measured up the rooms, sketched plans, argued, made all kinds of suggestions: 'What if the mistress of the house falls ill? Would she be comfortable in the room you have given her. This too would be very noisy because of this or that,' etc. The bedroom was changed and everything else had to be changed round accordingly. After a number of rehearsals we had settled the arrangement of the rooms more or less comfortably and began to 'live' in them. When the gong sounded, we all left our own rooms and went to the dining room. Dorinne served us, running up and down the stairs. Life was calm and peaceful. That was before Tartuffe arrived.

Family situations were created, such as the illness of the mistress of the house. This governed the behaviour of all the members of the household. So we met for dinner, went to our rooms afterwards or took a walk, aware that there was someone we all loved seriously ill in the house.

Then we tried out other circumstances or events such as 'Tartuffe's first appearance at the house'. No one knew what his real character was so we all took him for a real man of God. Tartuffe's behaviour did not initially arouse suspicion. He was the epitome of meekness and humility. Accordingly, everyone's attitude towards him was sympathetic. Against this background, we played out a series of interesting improvisations such as 'Tartuffe goes wild', or 'Orgon had lost his mind'. Our games had to be conducted with the same naive truth and sincerity which we find in children's games. We liked that. We were happy to go to rehearsal and play games. Sometimes they went well and we were pleased with ourselves, at other times they didn't work and we were annoyed: 'Here we are, grown-up people, playing silly children's games.'

In the theatre there were stories, some true, some untrue, about what we were doing. And we ourselves, although we went on with our work, and sometimes with great enthusiasm, were not entirely convinced of its usefulness. Yet the problems we set ourselves, and which the directors tried to solve, were of a creative nature, and we were heading the right way to achieve our goal. But we only understood that much later.

Stanislavski said:

'You are a large group of people on a boat. You're sitting up on deck, having lunch, eating, drinking, talking, flirting with the ladies. You do it all rather well. But is it art? No, it's life. Now, take another situation. You come to rehearsal. A deck has been set up on stage, a table is laid. You enter and ask yourselves, "If we were on a boat with a happy group of friends, what would we do?" And that's when your creative work begins.'

The subjects of our later games in Orgon's house grew ever closer to what we could remember of Molière's play: 'Mme Pernelle, Orgon's mother, in a rage, storms out of the house, terrifying the members of the family who try to prevent her.'

Or: 'Orgon directs his daughter to sign the marriage contract, while the rest of the family beg her not to do so.'

'Only, for mercy's sake, don't let's have any of Molière's actual lines or any set moves,' Stanislavski urged us.

Having worked for some time on some scenes we decided to show Stanislavski the results of our efforts. First, we showed him Madame Pernelle's departure, that is, the opening of the play. The cast used their own words following the general sense of the scene. We didn't play for long. After a very short time Stanislavski stopped the rehearsal.

'You're not behaving, you're just saying words, not the author's words, true, but you're so used to them they have become a script. They sound like something you have learned, only it's not as good as Molière. I don't need words but physical behaviour. What is the physical sequence of the events. Sit down, please, all of you. Listen carefully. The situation in Orgon's family is extremely tense. The master of the house has gone away, leaving his mother to look after Tartuffe. Orgon's mother worships this saintly person and what will her son think, on his return, if he learns she has decided to quit the family home, leaving Tartuffe alone? What an uproar there will be in the house, how Tartuffe will play on it, how much more difficult it will be to fight him. You must do everyhting you can to restrain and mollify this furious old woman, and she must not only refuse to give in to your arguments, she mustn't even let you open your mouths. If anyone tries to argue with her, she quickly demolishes him, insults him and kills any desire he has to continue the quarrel. This is Molière not Chekhov. Here uproar is uproar and a row is a row. So what is the physical sequence? What appeals to you?

'Imagine a cage full of very fierce tigers with their tamer. They are ready to tear him apart at any moment and he only controls them by keeping his eyes on them the whole time. He reads their intentions in their eyes and nips them in the bud. He does not give them a chance to do anything. If one of the tigers tries to attack him, he gives it such a whipping that it runs away, its tail between its legs. Remember, there's not just one tiger in the cage but five or six and every one of them ready to pounce if the tamer takes his eyes off them for one moment. So, what would you do? Try it, try it . . . But none of you is sitting in the right rhythm! Try to find the right rhythm! You, dear boy, you're not preparing for a fight, but to put your feet up and read the newspaper.' (The actor stood up.) 'No, don't stand up. You can be ready to spring even when you're sitting. So, let's see what you can do. No, that's not it . . . I am asking all of you, sitting there, to find the right inner rhythm. An angry rhythm. It can be seen in very tiny actions. No . . . no, that's not it . . . are you really incapable of doing simple things? Where's your technique. All we have to do is take away your script, your "protector", and everything goes. I want you to learn to *do*, to do physical actions. You will need words and ideas later on to reinforce and develop these actions. But right now I'm asking you to prepare for a fight. Is that so difficult for you?'

It really was difficult for us. We couldn't do what he wanted. And no matter how long Stanislavski fought with us the result was negative.

'Oh, oh oh! . . . You have no will. That's terrible! This is no way to work.'

We started to assure him that we did have will, that we really wanted to fulfil the task, but we couldn't do it because it was really all so unusual for us. We couldn't do anything sitting down and certainly not in an angry rhythm. It all came out false, we didn't believe what we were doing, we were in a muddle. We thought in fact that the whole thing was impossible.

'Absolute nonsense! Rhythm must be felt in the eyes, in tiny movements. These are elementary things. I am asking you to sit in a specific rhythm. To modify the rhythm of your behaviour. Any third-year student can do that.'

One of the actors, evidently caught on the raw, asked:

'And can *you* do it?'

We all froze. We waited for the storm, but Stanislavski immediately, almost without a pause, responded quietly:

'Of course. You want an angry rhythm. So.'

And, there and then, sitting on the sofa, in an instant he was transformed. We saw an extremely anxious person, someone on tenterhooks. He took out his watch, barely looked at it and put it back, then prepared to rise, but sat back down again, then he sat stock still, ready to pounce at any moment. He made a countless number of swift movements. Each of them was inwardly justified, and totally convincing. The display was wonderful and we were all in raptures over it, but he just went on with his exercise and after a little while quietly asked:

'Do you want me to continue in another rhythm?'

And he began again, but this time there was a totally calm, composed person, as it were, deciding to go to bed but putting the actual moment off. It was very convincing.

'But how are we to do this?'

'Through daily exercises. What you are doing now is very good but add work on rhythm to it. You can't master the method of physical action if you don't master rhythm. Each physical action is indissolubly linked to a characteristic rhythm. If you always do everything in your own personal rhythm, how will you be able to characterise different people?'

'But what if, as you say, I actually have a very lazy personal rhythm,' asked the same audacious actor. 'We are supposed to start from ourselves, from our own personal traits, aren't we? What if I have no idea what an angry rhythm is?'

'Well now . . . what if someone finds your sore spot? Do you stay in the same lazy rhythm?'

'Yes, but . . .'

'Your lazy rhythm exists until you are caught on the raw. In the play you are acting out events which, perhaps, don't produce that effect on you, as they should. But what if things were otherwise? Behave as if you, you personally, were caught on the raw. First, use the physical actions you have established as an impulse to further actions. But don't act them out, simply state: I can do this, but that I can't do yet. Respect the logical sequence of your actions and work through your role using your own, not the dramatist's words, and even when you read the script don't do so out loud. Work with quiet courage. Avoid self-criticism: "Oh hell, that's wrong!"

'What is belief on stage? You have to move in boldly, decisively, that is, with crystal-clear logic. The audience will watch what you do. And as you continue calmly you will become fascinated by your own working process, and that is partial belief. But to capture an audience, this partial belief must become total belief.'

With that the rehearsal ended. Stanislavski had once more turned his attention to the importance of rhythm and had let us go, although he was not entirely satisfied with the results of our work. In conversation with Kedrov, he complained about our lack of will, and even expressed the view that certain of us did not really want to go on working. Everyone had to be questioned about the purity of their motives.

We prepared for the next demonstration by taking stock of everything that had happened during the previous one. We did daily exercises on rhythm and achieved one or two results. We found the rhythm of the scene we were preparing to show. We deliberately chose another scene ('Orgon and the marriage contract'). It opens with the distraught members of the family, who have taken poor Marianne under their protection, discussing how to thwart Orgon's incredible decision to marry his daughter to Tartuffe. Orgon bursts into the room, contract in hand, during this stormy discussion.

We underlined certain words, '*distraught* members of the family', 'Orgon *bursts* into the room during this *stormy discussion*', as indicating the rhythm in which we were to behave in this particular case.

Before we started the scene, we explained at length and in detail to Stanislavski what we wanted to do, how *stormily* we discuss, how we are all *distraught*, how Orgon *bursts* in, how the relatives want to rebuff Orgon, etc., etc.

Stanislavski interrupted our explanations:

'In scenes like this, when actors start thinking, "we will rebuff him, we will do this and that," and so on, it merely weakens the will. Don't think about it, do it, rebuff him. So, what are you going to do?'

We did the scene and considered it not at all bad.

'And what was all that about? A stormy discussion? There's a madman with a knife running through the house, looking for his daughter so he can stab her and all you can do is have a "stormy discussion". You need to save her, not talk about it . . . This is theatre. What is the physical sequence here? Decide on that first. Where can the madman burst in? Concentrate all your attention on the door, or rather on the brass knob. At the same time, think where you can hide Marianne, argue, swear at each other, but don't forget your principal concern for one second – a madman running about the house with a knife. If he opens the door, it's too late. The slightest move of the doorknob and Marianne must be hidden in a flash, so that Orgon does not have the least suspicion that she is here. Now, what are you going to do?'

It all seemed very simple, like all Stanislavski's directions, and didn't require further explanation. But as soon as we began, we felt how far we were from getting it right, and that we couldn't give a hundredth part of what he wanted, even in our best renderings of the scene. It was all a repetition of quite clever but nonetheless theatrical clichés.

'All right, let's forget the play . . . it doesn't exist. There's no Orgon, no Marianne or anyone else. There is just you. Let's play a game. Toporkov will go out into the corridor and stand some distance from the door. All of you in the room try to decide where he is. No one in the room has the right to move from where they are until the doorknob moves and, as soon as it does, you hide Marianne wherever you like but try to do it before the door opens and Toporkov rushes in. He must not be able to see where Marianne has been hidden. And Toporkov, as he comes in, must say at once where she is. If he can't, he has lost, if he can, you have lost. So, please, begin the game while I talk to the directors.'

Stanislavski took off his pince-nez, to underline the fact that he wasn't watching us, then he consulted his notes and talked to the directors.

We began. Initially nothing worked. It was impossible to hide Marianne in such a short space of time. I rushed into the room when the others had only just managed to take hold of her, or even if they had hidden her, I could see where. But gradually, each time we did it, we began to get carried away. We called each other clumsy, we had slanging matches, and I suddenly wanted to win at all costs. When one of them said that apart from the doorknob, they should listen carefully for my approaching footsteps, I took off my shoes and worked in my socks. To be brief, we were so absorbed in the game that we forgot about Stanislavski and the directors, who had long since ended their discussion and were watching our excited game as though it were a football match. We didn't manage to hide Marianne. The circumstances were too difficult.

Stanislavski stopped us at the height of the game.

'This is no longer theatre. This is genuine, real-life action, full of concentration and commitment. That's what I need in this scene. You didn't perform it, but, after today's game, you now understand what lies behind these people's physical behaviour. You must believe in what you have just done, how you behaved, and try to find the same concentration, dynamism, truth, rhythm, everything that happened as a result of your involvement with the episode, in all later rehearsals. Don't think about the audience, there isn't one, it does not exist as far as you are concerned and the more completely you do that, the more attention it will pay to your actions, as we did just now. That is a law of the theatre.'

After these remarks, Stanislavski turned to the directors and said:

'Did you see how remarkably varied and unexpected the staging was during this game? You can't plan that in advance. It would be good if we could do it afresh each time. My dream is a performance in which the actors don't know which of the four sides the audience is on.'

Taking his leave, Stanislavski requested each of us to believe in, to prize everything that had happened in the rehearsal, and to try and perfect what we had discovered in the future.

'Bear in mind,' he said, 'that you cannot recall and set feelings, you can only recall a sequence of physical actions, make it strong, give it all the smoothness of habit. When you rehearse this scene, start with the simplest physical actions, perform them absolutely truthfully, look for truth in every detail. In this way you will achieve belief in yourself and what you are doing. Take account of everything that relates to your actions, especially rhythm, which, like everything else, is the result of the given circumstances of one kind or another. We know how to perform simple physical actions, but depending on the given circumstances, these physical actions become psychophysical.'

The rehearsals for *Tartuffe*, which had begun with what seemed like abstract exercises and various elements of acting technique, grew imperceptibly closer to Molière's play. We went on doing daily exercises and improvisations as a kind of preparatory cleaning-up process.

Our rehearsals had their own special character, but when he talked to us, Stanislavski sometimes touched on subjects he had previously avoided. True, when this happened, he quickly realised what he was doing, and tried to relate everything to the task he had set himself as a teacher, and so limit us to our attempts to look to the future.

Thus, one day we were discussing the two lead characters in the play, Orgon and Tartuffe, and the question arose: what are the special ways which Tartuffe uses to get such a complete hold on Orgon? How does he, as Stanislavski put it, 'bedazzle' him? He would have to do something very special to dupe a perfectly normal man like Orgon. If you think Orgon is an idiot who can be taken in by any kind of crude tomfoolery, then the play's not worth doing. No, a very subtle kind of art is required. Tartuffe is a dangerous swindler. He is dangerous precisely because he can delude far from foolish people and he has a whole battery of cunning ways of tricking them, and he varies them according to the nature of his current victim.

We know from the script that the first meeting between Orgon and Tartuffe takes place in church, and that Orgon was struck by the fervour with which Tartuffe was praying.

> He used to come into our church each day
> And humbly kneel nearby, and start to pray.
> He'd draw the eyes of everybody there
> By the deep fervour of his heartfelt prayer;

He'd sigh and weep, and sometimes with a sound
Of rapture he would bend and kiss the ground.

That is what he did, so as not to look like the usual religious hypocrite, and to find new ways of drawing attention to himself.

Or take another crucial moment, when Tartuffe is caught attempting to seduce Elmire. He has no hope of justifying himself and yet gets off scot-free. How does he do that? True, he has a very long speech in which he very cleverly confuses the whole issue, so at moments like these it is very difficult to get at the truth through all the high-flown phrases. The proof is obvious, and the husband is furious, the whole atmosphere is at white-heat. Yes or no, asks Orgon, and Tartuffe boldly replies, yes. And yet, I repeat, he gets off scot-free.

So, again, how does he do it? We might, of course, say that Orgon has such faith in Tartuffe that he sees this as just another plot by his family who are steeped in sin. He can believe anything, even that Tartuffe wanted to seduce Elmire for the highest motives, and is delighted by it. But we absolutely rejected that version of events. No, Orgon is not that stupid. He loves his wife, the evidence against Tartuffe is incontrovertible, and he goes into an indescribable rage. Tartuffe is presented with a complex task: to get out of a desperate situation. He can't do it by reason, not right at this moment, that might work later. He needs to be amazing, staggering, but how? We discussed this with Kedrov. We ran through all the sanctimonious people we knew in an attempt to understand how they influence people, and broached the subject in one of our rehearsals with Stanislavski.

'Absolutely right . . . So try now to astonish Toporkov . . . and really astonish him.'

'How can we astonish him? We know each other too well . . . It's very difficult.'

'Why? It isn't difficult at all. All you need is daring. Get up to some antics in front of me, in front of the others, something you would only do when you were alone. Don't think. Who's going to try?'

Nobody.

'This means you lack what I call barefaced cheek. That's something actors should cultivate.'

Half-joking, half-serious, somewhat shamefaced, we started to do exercises with Kedrov in 'barefaced cheek', trying to outdo each other in daring. Stanislavski didn't stop us, and one exercise turned into another and went on for some time. And the longer we went on, the more audacious and daring we became till finally we had gone as far as it was possible to go and stopped.

'That was very good. There are an infinite number of variations you can play . . .' Then, after he had recounted one or two interesting, vivid stories from his own life, he continued: 'Try to work out how you could stop someone who, in a state of rage, attacks you and wants to kill you on the spot. You need to act decisively, so don't be half-hearted. Don't think about the means you are going to use, only about your assailant and decide how you can stop him here, today. Tomorrow it might be quite different. Amaze, astonish Toporkov a new way each time. Otherwise he'll beat you with his stick.'

As a result of these exercises, Kedrov, who was playing Tartuffe, found a wonderful way of playing the scene with Orgon in Act Three. Trapped and guilty, he stands by the sofa in the middle of the room, Bible in hand, like an animal at bay, trying to find a way out. Approaching him slowly, stealthily like a enraged panther, his stick raised ready to strike, with biting sarcasm Orgon says:

– Can it be true, this dreadful thing I hear?

There is a tense, dreadful pause and then Tartuffe replies:

– Yes!

The stick is raised and suddenly . . . a piercing shriek is heard. Cleverly, invisibly, Tartuffe has kicked the sofa over, so that its legs are in the air, and Orgon's stick, to his astonishment, strikes the air. He drops the stick and looks around not understanding what has happened. Had there been a thunderbolt from heaven to punish him for blasphemy? He looks questioningly at Tartuffe, who pays no attention at all, but is on the floor kissing the stick Orgon has dropped and is talking privately to God who is somewhere up above. He seems to be asking God what to do with Orgon, forgive him or punish him? Tartuffe's position, his incomprehensible conversation with someone, cannot but make an impression on Orgon. He is confused, he doesn't know what to do, while Tartuffe, who has all his wits about him, begins to spin his web of words:

– Yes, Brother, I'm a wicked man, I fear.

Orgon listens. In the voice of this 'saint', he detects not only notes of repentance, but notes of outraged innocence. Then Orgon begins to realise that this repentance is for his general state of sin, and not for the present case, which is no more than a provocation by his enemies etc., etc.

Having warded off the first blow, it was easy for Tartuffe to manipulate Orgon and divert all his anger somewhere else.

Success was frequently mixed with failure. At times Stanislavski was saddened by the miserable results we showed him after a long period of work. He was not so much depressed by the degree of readiness or not of a particular scene, but by the degree to which we had or had not mastered his method. Once we played the famous scene in the third act (Orgon, Dorine, Marianne) not at all badly, but Stanislavski didn't even smile and at the end said, sadly: 'The scene is ready, you can play it at the Moscow Art Theatre. But you could have played it that way without me. That's not what I brought you here for. You're repeating what you know how to do already, but you have to move forward, and I am offering you a method for doing that. I thought it would make your task easier but you reject it, and want to go back to your old ways. So, go back to the Moscow Art Theatre and they will put on a play quickly for you.'

But, one way or another, finally we reached the next phase in rehearsal in which we needed the script. The patterns of action we had discovered and rehearsed needed to be given greater expression and completeness by thoughts and words. I don't remember if Stanislavski or one of the directors suggested that we pass on to a new phase. It just seemed to happen, gradually, out of a growing inner need. True, there were times when we went back to the earlier phase of our work. Before each rehearsal we continued to do our 'clean-up', but now we had other tasks, complex tasks which defined to some the degree the shape of a scene. In brief, we worked on the words. The 'impulses' to action we had worked on had to be developed and rounded out through active words. We had to make the characters come to grips with each other in a dynamic verbal conflict. We had been prepared for this by all our previous work, but Stanislavski's demands were so enormous that in this phase of our work we also felt misery. Stanislavski didn't let one empty phrase, one word that was not justified by an 'inner image' pass.

'Don't listen to yourselves, just see what it is you are talking about, as clearly and in as much minute detail as in life. It will then be clearer on stage and the audience will see it more clearly.'

That was the inner aspect, and the outer:

'Molière's characters are French, their feelings are strong, their thoughts clear as the stroke of a pen, they don't stop for explanations. They flow swift and easy. A thought is a sentence. And this is complicated by the fact that the play is in verse.'

None of us had really mastered the art of speaking verse or understood rhythm and scansion. But here, too, Stanislavski made enormous demands:

'The rhythm of the verse must live in the actor, when he is speaking and when he is silent. The whole performance must be charged with rhythm, then you can pause between words and phrases, and they all fall into the right rhythm.'

It was an agonisingly long time before I got the famous scene in Act One between Orgon and Dorine right. On his return from the country, Orgon questions Dorine about what has been happening in his house during his absence, learning all the details of his wife's dreadful illness, yet he keeps on asking the same question:

– Ah. And Tartuffe?

And despite the most reassuring reports over his favourite, he repeats, sometimes with alarm, sometimes with tender tears,

– Poor fellow!

five or six times in the course of the scene. I was deeply aware of the humour and charm of this scene, but could not convey it. However many different ways I found of saying 'Ah. And Tartuffe?' and 'Poor fellow!', the words were lifeless, and did not fit into the fine tracery of Dorine's speech. They hung in the air, heavy and unreal. I didn't believe in myself and was desperate. And as so often happens, the scene you like most when you read a play, the one in which you place your highest hopes, turns out to be the most difficult or doesn't work at all. This was the case now. Everyone sympathised with me, gave me advice on how I should play it. I could talk about it, but I couldn't play it . . .

'What's the problem?' asked Stanislavski, after I had helplessly gabbled through the scene.

'I don't know, I just feel that there's no way it can work. I realise the scene is witty and elegant but, when I try it, it is dull, clumsy and boring.'

'Hm! . . . Hm . . . I don't think you're really seeing it. You see the outside of the scene, its elegance, and that's what you're trying to play, but you need to direct your mind to your wife's bedroom, to Tartuffe's room, the place Dorine is telling you about and create "mental images". You're not listening to her. Try to understand what she is thinking. Listen to Dorine's story:

— Your wife fell ill.

Just listen. There's no need to move your hands or head. But your eyes, your trusting eyes, are drawing the whole event out of her:

— How are the family? What's been going on?

'You keep pausing before each word. Everything's in the muscles of your tongue. You don't have any "mental images", you don't know your own bedroom and, you must, in every detail.

— Your wife fell ill

'Your mind is in your bedroom where your wife in lying in a fever, no one in the house is sleeping, they are all rushing about. You have to see that. They send for the doctor, they bring ice, there is noise and bustle everywhere. But you think to yourself, right next to the bedroom is Tartuffe's cell where he talks to God. They are preventing him from praying. Your wife is forgotten, everything under the sun is forgotten, you must know about Tartuffe at once. "Ah. And Tartuffe?"

'That's what you must work on. Don't think about the way you are going to say your lines. Listen to Dorine, really listen closely, and imagine what might be happening to Tartuffe under these circumstances. To your question:

— Ah. And Tartuffe?

Dorine replies:

— [He] zealously devoured in her presence / A leg of mutton and a brace of pheasants.

'Dear heaven! How he must have worn himself out in the night to work up such an extraordinary appetite:

— Poor fellow!

'You listen to what she is saying and make your own assumptions, which are not in the script, but result in the script.

The secret of the scene lies in a capacity to listen. Dorine, for her part, must take note of your reaction to each of her lines, and throw in this or that accordingly. She must discern your thoughts through your eyes. She is very clever and, in any case, knows you very well. So there is a parallel dialogue to the script. If you combine the script with your unspoken thoughts then we get (Molière's text is in italics):

> DORINE: *She thanked us all for everything.*[1]
> ORGON: Thank God, all is well. I can imagine how joyful everyone was. But in their happiness they forgot poor Tartuffe, who undoubtedly restored her. They probably didn't even feed him, poor man, and he sat humbly in his cell, alone.
> DORINE: Aha, I see he is worried about his holy man.
> ORGON: *Ah. And Tartuffe?*
> DORINE: I knew it! Just you wait, I'll have you!
> *Knowing how much strength Madame had lost*
> Aha, now you're really upset.
> *He made it good at once.*
> ORGON: Heaven. What did he do? Give his blood! Or what! For heaven's sake, quick . . .
> DORINE: Ah, you want to know what sacrifice he made. I'm sorry you're such a fool you haven't yet understood.
> *Two extra stoops of wine he gladly emptied*
> *For his breakfast.*
> ORGON: Dear heaven, but he doesn't drink. How much he loves us all! He was so full of joy he damaged his own health.
> *Poor man!*

'Of course, you mustn't be too ponderous here. French temperament is such that thoughts flash through their minds, they clearly understand a situation in all its subtlety and work it out as they go.

'But don't forget the intricate pattern of thoughts that led up to your speaking this line. Remember, people only speak ten per cent of what is in their heads, ninety per cent remains unspoken. In the theatre, people forget this, they only care about what is spoken out loud, and destroy living truth.

'When you are doing a scene, you must, first and foremost,

---

[1] This line is not in Molière's original. The Russian translation is fairly free. I follow the Russian version here to match the inner monologue Stanislavski describes.

establish all the thoughts that precede any given line. You don't have to speak them, just live them. You can, perhaps, rehearse for a while speaking everything out loud, so that you can master your own and the other actor's unspoken lines and the exchange of thoughts so that your unspoken thoughts can be in accord with his.

'In the scene you have just shown me the most important thing to learn is to listen, especially Orgon, and to guess what your partner's hidden thoughts are. Then classic lines like "Ah. And Tartuffe?" and "Poor man!" fall into place automatically. You don't have to think about them. And Dorine, don't forget that she has set this up as a performance for Cléante's benefit, so that she can give him a concrete example of the truth of what she has been saying. "The girl was laughing in your face," Cléante says to Orgon on Dorine's exit. Do you know what your task is? To provoke him so he behaves the way you want.

'You must be fully aware of these elements in your behaviour and rehearse not what is in the lines, but what is between them. Bendina [playing Dorine] must work out, before each rehearsal, ways of provoking Toporkov, of tricking him, so that he always falls for it. That is the moment when Dorine will understand the nature of what she has to do in this scene with Orgon.

'You wanted to be able to play this scene without preparing the way for it, without ordering or disciplining your thoughts, your inner images. You wanted quick results, to pluck them out of the air. It all seems so simple but, as you see, you failed. Of course, you might have succeeded, but since you didn't, I'm giving you a way to overcome your difficulties. It really is a very difficult scene. Remember, it is a classic example of Molière's comedies.

'Once he has obtained all he needs to know from Dorine about the situation at home, Orgon dismisses his servant and remains alone with his brother-in-law, Cléante. They have a lengthy conversation. Cléante begins carefully, but then explains more and more openly all that is wrong with Orgon's family life since Tartuffe appeared. Orgon, on the other hand, assures Cléante that it is only since this saintly man came among them that his family has begun to live a beautiful, pious, life that is pleasing to God.

'Both express their opinions in long speeches. The scene has a "conversational" character. That is the way it is usually played: one delivers his speech and the other waits and vice versa. One speaks his lines passionately, energetically, the other is cooler, more rational – but all that is nothing more than word-spinning. This scene is played inevitably, as in every play, as boring exposition, and, unfortunately, it closes the act. When an audience loses interest at the end of an act, it is always, naturally, bad for the show. How are we to raise this scene to the level of the turbulent events that have preceded it? Not only to their level but much higher? That is what our job is about.'

SCENE FIVE: *Orgon, Cléante*[1]

CLEANTE: That girl was laughing in your face, and though
I've no wish to offend you, even so
I'm bound to say that she had some excuse.
How can you possibly be such a goose?
Are you so dazed by this man's hocus-pocus
That all the world, save him, is out of focus?
You've given him clothing, shelter, food, and care;
Why must you also . . .
ORGON: Brother, stop right there.
You do not know the man of whom you speak.
CLEANTE: I grant you that. But my judgment's not so weak
That I can't tell, by his effect on others . . .
ORGON: Ah, when you meet him, you two will be like brothers!
There's been no loftier soul since time began.
He is a man who . . . a man who . . . an excellent man.
To keep his precepts is to be reborn,
And view this dunghill of a world with scorn.
Yes, thanks to him I'm a changed man indeed.
Under his tutelage my soul's been freed
From earthly loves, and every human tie:
My mother, children, brother, and wife could die,
And I'd not feel a single moment's pain.
CLEANTE: That's a fine sentiment, Brother; most humane.
ORGON: Oh, had you seen Tartuffe as I first knew him,
Your heart, like mine, would have surrendered to him.
He used to come into our church each day
And humbly kneel nearby, and start to pray.
He'd draw the eyes of everybody there
By the deep fervour of his heartfelt prayer;
He'd sigh and weep, and sometimes with a sound
Of rapture he would bend and kiss the ground;

[1] Act I scene vi in the original.

And when I rose to go, he'd run before
To offer me holy-water at the door.
His serving-man, no less devout than he,
Informed me of his master's poverty;
I gave him gifts, but in his humbleness
He'd beg me every time to give him less.
'Oh, that's too much,' he'd cry, 'too much by twice!
I don't deserve it. The half, Sir, would suffice.'
And when I wouldn't take it back, he'd share
Half of it with the poor, right then and there.
At length, Heaven prompted me to take him in
To dwell with us, and free our souls from sin.
He guides our lives, and to protect my honour
Stays by my wife, and keeps an eye upon her;
He tells me whom she sees, and all she does,
And seems more jealous than I ever was!
And how austere he is! Why, he can detect
A mortal sin where you would least suspect;
In smallest trifles, he's extremely strict.
Last week, his conscience was severely pricked
Because, while praying, he had caught a flea
And killed it, so he felt, too wrathfully.
CLEANTE: Good God, man! Have you lost your
common sense –
Or is this all some joke at my expense?
How can you stand there and in all sobriety . . .
ORGON: Brother, your language savours of impiety.
Too much free-thinking's made your faith unsteady,
And as I've warned you many times already,
'Twill get you into trouble before you're through.
CLEANTE: So I've been told before by dupes like you:
Being blind, you'd have all others blind as well;
The clear-eyed man you call an infidel,
And he who sees through humbug and pretence
Is charged, by you, with want of reverence.
Spare me your warnings, Brother; I have no fear
Of speaking out, for you and Heaven to hear,
Against affected zeal and pious knavery.
There's true and false in piety, as in bravery,
And just as those whose courage shines the most
In battle, are the least inclined to boast,

So those whose hearts are truly pure and lowly
Don't make a flashy show of being holy.
There's a vast difference, so it seems to me,
Between true piety and hypocrisy:
How do you fail to see it, may I ask?
Is not a face quite different from a mask?
Cannot sincerity and cunning art,
Reality and semblance, be told apart?
Are scarecrows just like men, and do you hold
That a false coin is just as good as gold:
Ah, Brother, man's a strangely fashioned creature
Who seldom is content to follow Nature,
But recklessly pursues his inclination
Beyond the narrow bounds of moderation,
And often, by transgressing Reason's laws,
Perverts a loftly aim or noble cause.
A passing observation, but it applies.
ORGON: I see, dear Brother, that you're profoundly wise;
You harbour all the insight of the age.
You are our one clear mind, our only sage,
The era's oracle, its Cato too,
And all mankind are fools compared to you.
CLEANTE: Brother, I don't pretend to be a sage,
Nor have I all the wisdom of the age.
There's just one insight I would dare to claim:
I know that true and false are not the same;
And just as there is nothing I more revere
Than a soul whose faith is steadfast and sincere,
Nothing that I more cherish and admire
Than honest zeal and true religious fire,
So there is nothing that I find more base
Than specious piety's dishonest face –
Than these bold mountebanks, these histrios
Whose impious mummeries and hollow shows
Exploit our love of Heaven, and make a jest
Of all that men think holiest and best;
These calculating souls who offer prayers
Not to their Maker, but as public wares,
And seek to buy respect and reputation
With lifted eyes and sighs of exaltation;
These charlatans, I say, whose pilgrim souls

Proceed, by way of Heaven, toward earthly goals,
Who weep and pray and swindle and extort,
Who preach the monkish life, but haunt the court,
Who make their zeal the partner of their vice –
Such men are vengeful, sly, and cold as ice,
And when there is an enemy to defame
They cloak their spite in fair religion's name,
Their private spleen and malice being made
To seem a high and virtuous crusade,
Until, to mankind's reverent applause,
They crucify their foe in Heaven's cause.
Such knaves are all too common; yet, for the wise,
True piety isn't hard to recognise,
And, happily, these present times provide us
With bright examples to instruct and guide
Consider Ariston and Périandre;
Look at Oronte, Alcidamas, Clitandre;
Their virtue is acknowledged; who could doubt it?
But you won't hear them beat the drum about it.
They're never ostentatious, never vain,
And their religion's moderate and humane;
It's not their way to criticise and chide:
They think censoriousness a mark of pride,
And therefore, letting others preach and rave,
They show, by deeds, how Christians should behave.
They think no evil of their fellow man,
But judge of him as kindly as they can.
They don't intrigue and wangle and conspire;
To lead a good life is their one desire;
The sinner wakes no rancorous hate in them;
It is the sin alone which they condemn;
Nor do they try to show a fiercer zeal
For Heaven's cause than Heaven itself could feel.
These men I honour, these men I advocate
As models for us all to emulate.
Your man is not their sort at all, I fear:
And, while your praise of him is quite sincere,
I think that you've been dreadfully deluded.
ORGON: Now then, dear Brother, is your speech concluded?
CLEANTE: Why, yes.
ORGON: Your servant, Sir. (*He turns to go.*)

CLEANTE: No, Brother; wait.
There's one more matter. You agreed of late
That young Valère might have your daughter's hand.
ORGON: I did.
CLEANTE: And set the date, I understand.
ORGON: Quite so.
CLEANTE: You've now postponed it; is that true?
ORGON: No doubt.
CLEANTE: The match no longer pleases you?
ORGON: Who knows?
CLEANTE: D'you mean to go back on your word?
ORGON: I won't say that.
CLEANTE: Has anything occurred
Which might entitle you to break your pledge?
ORGON: Perhaps.
CLEANTE: Why must you hem, and haw, and hedge?
The boy asked me to sound you in this affair . . .
ORGON: It's been a pleasure.
CLEANTE: But what shall I tell Valère?
ORGON: Whatever you like.
CLEANTE: But what have you decided?
What are your plans?
ORGON: I plan, Sir, to be guided
By Heaven's will.
CLEANTE: Come, Brother, don't talk rot.
You've given Valère your word; will you keep it, or not?
ORGON: Good day.
CLEANTE: This looks like poor Valère's undoing;
I'll go and warn him that there's trouble brewing.

No! This is not, of course, a rational discussion between two men of reason.[1] It is not an academic disputation. It is a life-and-death struggle between two protagonists. Some incident, perhaps, stayed Orgon's hand at the last minute and stopped him committing murder (the blasphemous Cléante, nonetheless, will not escape the wrath of heaven). While one of the opponents is delivering his speech, the other doesn't just wait, oh no! They are like men on tenterhooks. Every word they speak grates on the other's nerves.

[1] The 'man of reason', the 'raisonneur', was a standard character in the comedy of Molière's time. Cléante is a perfect example of the 'raisonneur' always presenting a middle common-sense path.

After this struggle, two relatives become mortal enemies. This is the turning point of the play. From this moment Orgon's relationship to his relatives and family enters a new phase, the struggle between the two sides becomes more acute. Orgon has decided to give his only daughter in marriage to Tartuffe and so deprive his enemies of their weapons.

We came to this conclusion after working in detail on the scene. However, to come to a conclusion was one thing; we also had to make it work. How were we to plan this scene? All the decisions we made were still very much 'in general'. Yes, there was a life-and-death struggle but what did it consist of? What were the individual links in the chain? What is the concrete task of each of the protagonists? What kind of fight would it be? What was the sequence of physical actions? Etc., etc. And how were we to embody all this in practical terms, how were we to train ourselves? We worked as best we could with Kedrov who gave us very useful, shrewd pointers, and when we achieved a few results we went to Leontievski Lane for further instruction.

As was to be expected, the first thing to which Stanislavski drew our attention was the need to perfect the physical behaviour of the two protagonists, which we had to a certain extent discovered. We analysed 'walking on hot coals' and presented it in all kinds of variations. We developed the whole pattern of the fight between the furious relatives in detail without speaking the lines with the exception of any that spontaneously came out during rehearsal. The most important thing for us was the characters' physical behaviour. One of us jumped up from his seat and held the other down in his chair (not physically, or course, but by inner force). The one sitting in the chair is like a trapped beast, ready to pounce at any moment. He is waiting for the right moment to grab his enemy by the throat and claw him to pieces. The other, having attacked him, makes it clear he has said everything he wants and further exchanges no longer interest him. He sits calmly in his chair and picks up a newspaper. This enrages his opponent even more. He sets his imagination to work trying to make him lose patience but doesn't succeed. His enemy's cold indifference is unshakeable. Yet for all the calm attitude of his upper body, the tip of his boot is beginning to tap very slightly. That's his true rhythm. Eventually he sends his paper flying into a corner of the room, he jumps up, as if he's been stung, and the two protagonists stand eyeball to eyeball like fighting cocks.

Rehearsing in this way, we managed to discover a great deal of significant material which went into the final production. However, most of our discoveries, which had shown us the way to play the scene, were not subsequently used. The fight led us on to more restrained, civilised forms which did not weaken but rather heightened the inner tension.

'In the end Cléante surrenders,' one actor remarked. 'His overall action is one of gradual surrender.'

'The result is surrender, but the action itself is "I don't want to surrender",' Stanislavski responded.

Once we had understood the pattern of physical behaviour in the scene, we had to learn to deal with the words. That required unremitting creative effort. Cléante's rhetorical speeches are difficult because you need to devote all your time to making them not appear rhetorical, and when he is delivering his passionate speeches, Orgon must be equal to the vivid, rich humour of Molière's writing.

Of course, Stanislavski began as usual with the basics.

'Pay regular attention to your speech, your articulation, every day, every hour and not just for fifteen minutes every five days. In speech class you speak properly for fifteen minutes, but for the remaining one hundred and nineteen hours and forty-five minutes in daily life, you don't. That's nonsense. Verbal action is an actor's ability to touch another actor with his mental images. And to do that you have to see everything you are talking about in crystal-clear detail, so that he sees it that way too. Verbal action is very wide in its range. You can convey thought through your inflexions, exclamations, words. Conveying thoughts – that is action too. Your thoughts, words, inner images exist for the other actor. And what do you do? You, Toporkov, have just played a scene with one eye on the audience. You were aware of them the whole time. That shouldn't be. You should focus on your partner. What are you aiming for in this scene?'

'To convince Cléante . . .'

'So, you see the expression in his eyes, the way he looks at you. Try to change that expression, try to make it brighter. What do you need to do? You have to convey your inner images, you have to make him see things through your eyes. Don't speak for his ears, but for his eyes. You can threaten, flatter, beg, whatever you like. Only you do it for him, your partner and no one else. See the results of what you are doing by the expression in his eyes, don't let anything mentally come between you. True, you can't avoid it. The audience is always a draw. You have to be able to drag yourself away from them and return to your object. When you say the line, "Oh, had you seen Tartuffe as I had seen him," there's a pause after the "Oh". Why the pause there? That's ham. You did it for youself, not Cléante. What is Orgon trying to say? "If you had met Tartuffe as I did, you would be his friend too." You *would have been a friend* and not an enemy, that's what Orgon is trying to say. So why would he make a nonsensical pause after the word "Oh"? You thought that up to embellish the line. You were listening to hear how well it sounded. Never pre-plan a word or an action. You'll have self-consciousness, not intuition. The only thing you can do in advance is prepare your powers of concentration, and perform the creative 'clean-up' I have spoken of. You must speak complete thoughts. Only your partner can decide whether they are convincing or not. You can tell from his eyes, from his expression whether you have succeeded or not. If you haven't, find something else, new mental images, use a change of mood or tone. The only person who can judge whether what I am doing on stage is right or not is my partner. I can't do that for myself. The most important thing when working on a role is mental images. You say, "What if you, like me, were to meet Tartuffe?" Do you really know how you met him? Can you tell me in detail — the layout of the church, where you first saw Tartuffe at prayer, what was the interior like, etc., etc., in a word everything that made such an impression on you? Unless you can see all that, you won't be able to find the dynamism, the mood, the energy to convince Cléante. Your actions are only convincing and organic when you have concrete, detailed inner images. Otherwise your attempts to convince seem forced and tacked on and they will annoy the audience.

'You don't deliberately have to work yourself up into the ecstatic, naive, obsessive love Orgon has for Tartuffe. You cannot force feelings. Create the story of this obsession down to the smallest detail, leave absolutely nothing out. Your imagination needs to get to work. The story needs to be packed with gripping events and touching details. Your inner images of Tartuffe must contain all that is best in humankind. Create the picture of someone unique. You must see him crystal-clear. Perhaps it is someone you revere, who is or was alive, like, say, Leo Tolstoy. When you make up your story, picture a saintly man. Then try to create a picture for your partner. Splash out with a range of colours, change them, make them a constant surprise. That will also define the rhythm of the scene. If you fail, it means you aren't seeing properly, you need to change your inner images of Tartuffe because the Tartuffe you are now seeing is either too insignificant or is not precious to Orgon, so that there is nothing to say. Remember, with Molière, as with Gogol, there is not a single moment that isn't white-hot. That means that if you want to tell the story of Tartuffe praying, you must put all your energy, all your fire into it. That is only possible when you find a theme for your story that can light this fire. Look at the story of the flea that Molière introduces as a typical example. Orgon says:

> Last week, his conscience was severely pricked
> Because, while praying, he had caught a flea
> And killed it, so he felt, too wrathfully.

'Can you really see this picture of Tartuffe's goodness and tender-heartedness? How he jumped out of bed in the middle of the night, stark naked, shivering with cold, lit a candle and told his servant, Laurence,[1] of the disaster that had occurred, how they both looked for the flea for a long time, how Tartuffe, having found it, warmed it with his breath, trying to revive it, how he then put it on a clean sheet of paper and spent the night in prayer and bitter tears. That's the kind of picture, or something like it, you should see with your inner eye when you try to make Cléante feel reverence for this saintly man.

'And I tell you once more, and once more again, this is all for Cléante's benefit. Shake him, either by fear or tears, whichever you find better. If that doesn't work, colour the lines differently, adapt – and don't think about the way you are saying them. You shouldn't speak in single sentences but paint an entire picture. Don't break Venus into pieces but show her whole. The audience is a distraction. You have to engage your partner with rhythm and clear inner images. That's why it is terrible when an actor's will is weak. Direct all your energy to changing Cléante's attitude to Tartuffe. You are playing chess with him. You don't know what his moves will be, but take account of the essentials – his voice, inflexions, eyes, every movement of his muscles. Your partner should tell you which way to go. This then becomes genuine action.

[1] There is no such character in Molière's play.

'Now imagine: here we have Orgon doing this and Cléante listening more and more attentively as Orgon continues. Orgon is now convinced that he has set the godless Cléante on the right path and, when he has finished his story about the flea, he looks at him triumphantly, but Cléante simply states, "Good God, man, have you lost your common sense?" Do you know what that means for Orgon? That is what Molière's comedy is about. You have to play this scene afresh each time, forget the old methods you are so fond of, or it will merely turn into a virtuoso display of acting. What I want is living, organic action each time. Remember your task, nothing else: each of you is absolutely convinced he is in the right and wants, passionately, come what may, to make the other accept his beliefs, right away. Solve this problem here, today, now. Transmit your inner images to each other. One sees Tartuffe as saintly, shedding tears for a dead flea, the other sees him as a crook, planning to butcher the entire family. So you clash, head on.'

When working on this scene, Stanislavski at times reverted to the pattern of physical actions; at others he was concerned solely with the words, making us repeat this or that line, so that the sound was clear. Although he tested out our inner images, he kept going back to the sequence of physical actions.

'You talk about "persuading". Is that a psychological or a physical action?'

Or, turning to Cléante:

'You say listening to Orgon is distasteful. That isn't an action, it's a state of mind. What is the physical action here? It is possible "not to listen", there's a simple physical action for you. Showing "cold indifference" is another. How will you do this? There are a thousand different things you can do, but you can't plan them in advance in each specific case. The important thing is to be able to dismiss or encourage. This is how you will behave if you don't want to listen, appear indifferent and at the same time belittle everything coming from your partner. At first, you do what people usually do, listen closely, with interest, you then do the opposite. Your behaviour sets the tone for your partner's behaviour, every change in your position is his cue.'

We did what Stanislavski suggested. I spoke the same speech to different responses from Cléante; sometimes he listened, quietly encouraging me to be even more open; other times he would deliberately discount all my passionate words, yawning or getting involved in a newspaper that was lying on the table, or whistling a happy little tune. In a third situation, Cléante seemed ready to interrupt Orgon at any minute, and embark on a thunderous speech. Then he switched between all three attitudes during the speech in any order. These exercises were very useful. Having to watch Cléante the whole time, I forgot Stanislavski and his directorial eye. I found it easy to believe in myself and in my actions, I became dynamic, especially in those moments when I had to attract Cléante's attention and not allow him to interrupt me. There was a clearer, more unexpected range of tone and inflexion.

However, Stanislavski was still not satisfied and demanded an ever greater variety of tone and a broader range of adaptations.

'Remember, human adaptations and ways of expressing feeling are innumerable and almost never straightforward. Enthusiasm isn't always expressed by enthusiasm, but often by something that looks like the direct opposite: "How splendid this actor is!" You can express the greatest of enthusiasm in tones of outrage, tenderness, contempt, etc., but it is still the same feeling.'

Stanislavski demonstrated all these examples wonderfully. He then made me repeat several times the part of my speech in which I was especially in raptures over Tartuffe in different ways – with outrage, contempt, tenderness, despair, in a warning, a mocking, a sorrowful tone, etc., etc. But they all had to be the expression of Tartuffe's loftiness of soul:

> There's been no loftier soul since time began.
> He is a man who . . . a man who . . . an excellent man.
> To keep his precepts is to be reborn,
> And view this dunghill of a world with scorn.
> Yes, thanks to him I'm a changed man indeed.

Sometimes, as I spoke the first two lines with enthusiasm, I would receive a brief command from Stanislavski:
'Indignation!'
And I changed tone.
Stanislavski then commanded:
'Despair!'
And I changed to despair, etc.
This was a scene that interested Stanislavski greatly. He worked steadily on it, for a long time, first, because he considered it

important for the play, second, because it provided a good basis for technical exercises.

It seems to me that Stanislavski went through all the elements of his system when working with us. Once, he paid special attention to moments of human communication.

'What is wrong with you today? There is no communication, no object of attention. Communication comes and goes, or the object is too ponderous for a French play.'

Stanislavski often regretted the fact that actors ignore this vital living process, don't study it, don't know all the tiny links, and particularly the most essential aspect, the moment preceding action when not only humans, but animals, find their bearings. He often told us:

'Look at the way a dog comes into a room. What does he do first? He comes in, sniffs the air and then decides where his master is. He goes to him, gets his attention, and only then starts "talking" to him. It is the same with human beings, only much more varied and subtle.

'But what do actors do? They enter, do the moves, go where they are supposed to go, suddenly start a conversation without bothering to know whether the others are ready to listen to them. Replace a woman by a man and they won't even notice, they will tell the man they love him. If you don't find your bearings first, the organic, living process is destroyed. The actor lies, he doesn't believe in his own actions and falls into clichéd "acting". Only by obeying all the subtleties of real behaviour can an actor achieve an awareness of truth on stage and contact his own organic capacity to create.

'What are the elements of communication?

1) finding your bearings, 2) looking for your object, 3) concentrating on it, 4) sounding it out, 5) inner images, i.e., making someone see with your eyes, 6) never thinking about the way you say the words, thinking, rather, about your inner images, i.e., how best to convey both them and the events.

'You just played a scene of an angry exchange between two people. You went straight into it. You left out an essential preparatory phase – finding your bearings, sounding each other out, adapting to each other, establising the "radio waves" which will make it easier for you to begin this pernickety discussion. These subtleties, these tiny physical actions, occur partly before, partly during the first five or six lines, and are the first links in the scene's chain of action. Leave them out and you destroy the truth.

One man goes to another and asks for a favour. But before he gets to the point, even before he has spoken a single word, one of them had already decided on his chances of success, while the other has guessed the purpose of this approach. This is the result of a rapid summing-up of the situation, homing in, sounding each other out, observing each other's actions and behaviour closely. After an exchange of pleasantries, keeping the kind of distance that makes discussion easier, having studied all the circumstances and seen what mood the other is in, one of them comes to the point, his business or his request.

'All these psychological subtleties are undoubtedly present in normal human contact. You cannot ignore them in acting, they are decisive for us. They persuade both actor and audience of the genuineness, the truth of what is happening on stage. These subtleties form an important part of our technique, the technique of experiencing. Your quarrel scene should begin with you sounding each other out, studying each other. It builds to a climax and ends with a complete break. Only if you do it that way will the audience follow your quarrel with unwavering attention, and remain in a state of tension until its logical conclusion. If you destroy the basic logic, the audience will stop believing you, and may lose interest, and you will only be able to win their attention back by once again observing all the subtle logic of human communication. You can't just be a stage presence, you have to work on your craft, you must speak, behave. When you enter, your first line must set the tone. By the fourth or fifth line you must determine: "Here I'm behaving, here I'm playacting, here I'm just a stage presence, here I am truly alive." Then it is essential to establish genuine contact. Good! Now we have to get the breathing and the voice right. Right, good.

'An actor must be able to tell whether his performance is good or bad. He must be calm about it, not in an emotional fog. What do we need on stage? Focus plus sensitivity, and concentration on the given circumstances. That is the necessary precondition for producing the creative state. This occurs when you have belief plus truth. You reach the "I am being" through these two elements. You will then behave truthfully. On stage you have to be able to distinguish between: "Here I am lying, here I am truthful, here I am behaving, here I am static, here I am thinking about the audience, here I am being natural."

'There are theatres that adore lying, they cultivate it. Others fear lies. I have to tell you: don't be afraid of lies, they are a test of truth. You don't need to cultivate them but you don't need to be afraid of them either.

'I have never played a single role that didn't start with clichés. When I felt absolutely calm and thought I was playing like a god, it meant I was playing clichés and the purpose of my creative activity was the thought, "I am playing like a god." Often actors try, come what may, to be good, but that is unattainable, inconceivable. You have to go on stage to behave, not to act and to conquer. You can't "act" calmness. There must be truth in calmness. You can't act feelings, passions, actions in a generalised way, you have to behave according to nature. And another thing: the less you try, the better you reach your audience. What does "try harder" mean? It means trying to woo the audience, that the audience is your object. That is one of an actor's greatest vices. It is better not to notice the audience than to "woo" it.'

Passing on from questions of acting technique to our performance, Stanislavski placed special value on firming up individual scenes, defining the characters, the basic ideas of the play, showing us ways of achieving a more profound interpretation.

'We have to avoid the usual actors' approach to Molière, when there aren't real people on stage but very well-known "Molière" characters, stock figures. That's dreadful, boring and unconvincing, always. To imagine that an amusing comedy should be played this way is a harmful preconception. You must believe in the truth of the dramatic events and put yourselves in the characters' place. Drama, comedy, tragedy do not exist for an actor. There is Me, a person in the given circumstances. You decide what has happened: Rasputin has settled in Orgon's house and disrupts family life. The basic action of the play for all the characters, except Orgon and his mother, is to get rid of Tartuffe/Rasputin. For Orgon and his mother, on the other hand, it is to receive Tartuffe once and for all into the bosom of the family and submit the rest of their lives to his will. The action of the play revolves round this bitter struggle, and each character behaves and fights consistent with his own logic.

'Remember, on stage a shout doesn't denote strength but weakness. Vocal strength is the result of finding an overpowering, intuitive impulse which produces truthful adaptations and vocal colours! "Forte" is not "piano" and "piano" is not "forte", and that's that. But they are not mutually exclusive.

'The actor playing Orgon must not think of the comedy in his role. Comedy and humour arise from the course of the events. For Orgon, everything that happens is a real tragedy. If you think that through properly, and put yourself in his place, then your thinking might be, for example: "I have come across a man through whom I can surely have direct contact with God himself. I sincerely believe that. I want my family's well-being, I love them, I want to create a happy, beautiful life for them, I have brought a genuinely saintly man into my home. This is my greatest achievement, this is the turning point towards a bright future, and only a blind man wouldn't see it." But not only do they not see this as a special blessing and a gift from heaven, they begin a vile persecution of this messenger of God and they try blasphemously to defame him and throw him out of the house.

Orgon tries, with great sincerity, to reason with his nearest and dearest, to save them from the wrath of heaven, to save their mortal souls. He breaks with his wife, his brother-in-law, throws his son out of the house and disowns him. Then suddenly, while he is under the table, he realises he has made a fatal error. He has taken in not Leo Tolstoy or Jesus Christ, but a crook. Isn't that a tragedy?

'The climax of Molière's comedy is the scene in which Orgon emerges from under the table where he has heard the love scene between his wife and Tartuffe, and speaks the remarkable line: "That man's a perfect monster, I admit it!"

'Usually the actor playing Orgon tries to get a large, derisory laugh at this point. But if you, Toporkov, manage to provoke not laughter but genuine sympathy, then it will be a triumph. Think carefully about the deeper meaning of the play, look at the events not with an actor's, but with a real man's eyes. Put yourself in Orgon's place, draw close all those who are dear to you in the play – your wife, daughter, son and the others – love them and realise that you are watching them go to their perdition, and what it means to break off all connection to them. How strong your belief in Tartuffe's saintliness must be, if you, nonetheless, take that path. If you take all this into account, and fully understand it, you will feel your energy being fuelled and realise the depth of feeling you can reach when you are defending Tartuffe. These are passions of Shakespearean proportions. You want Tartuffe's attention. To gain the attention of a simple man is one thing, but to gain Christ's attention is another, hence your depth of feeling. It is fully justified especially when Christ comes into your home. Do you know what that means for a believer? That's what you must understand, that is Orgon's tragedy. The comic side will emerge on its own, out of the incongruity of your behaviour with regard to what is really going on in your home. An awareness of the humour of your situation will come to you. Don't worry about it, deal with other things. Try to get inside Orgon's mind, judge every event from his point of view. Experience this as tragedy, and you will come to high comedy. This is not the stubbornness of a fool, but of someone defending all that is best and brightest in his life, or life itself. The more these ideas, these inner images become part of you, the richer you will make the role and the more acutely, the more pitilessly you will brand the vile sin of hypocrisy. That is the goal of our production, its supertask, the theme of Molière's play.

'But don't try to do everything at once. It will be beyond you, you will overstrain. When you are rehearsing, gradually prepare the path for take-off, make the sequence of physical actions smooth and easy, develop and enrich them with your inner images. You can play the whole thing as a funny story, but what would be the point of a production like that? To amuse an admiring audience? Is that what theatre is about? Every production we make must be based on an idea. Apart from performing the play, and following the storyline, we must never, at any time, lose sight of the supertask.

'I remember when we went on tour to Petersburg. We rehearsed many times in the theatre we had been given. Sometimes rehearsals went on till two or three in the morning. Once I came out of the theatre, very tired, to go back to my hotel and rest, and was surprised at what met my eyes. There was a heavy frost outside. In the darkness, here and there, was the glow of bonfires. The whole square was filled with people. Some were warming themselves at the bonfires, others rubbing their hands, legs and ears, others still were standing about, arguing heatedly. There was the glow of the bonfires and the murmur of a thousand voices. I had no idea what was going on, and asked someone standing nearby, "What's this all about?" "They're waiting for tickets for your performance." "Dear God," I thought, "what a responsbility we have to satisfy the spiritual needs of these people, who are freezing all night, what great ideas and thoughts we must bring to them!"

'So, do you think we can allow ourselves to pay our debt to them by telling them a funny little story?! It took me a long time to get to sleep that night because of my heavy sense of responsibility.

It came to me that apart from the supertask of a play, there should be a super-supertask. I could not yet define it, but that night I felt that the people I saw in that square deserved much more than what we had brought them. The audience must see themselves in Orgon. They can genuinely laugh, here and there, when they remember the ludicrous situations into which he falls because of his credulity, his carelessness. They can reflect, here and there, curse themselves, be indignant at the vileness of parasites, who build their happiness on the weaknesses of those near them. They can even weep in places, but it is still comedy. The comedy, as comedy, is just given a little bite, and the audience leaves the theatre enriched.'

On External Characterisation

Stanislavski did not omit one single element of acting technique in his work with us. If, in the first period, we concentrated exclusively on physical action, later we worked with the same painstaking thoroughness on other aspects of acting: words, rhythm, thoughts, inner images, verse-speaking, etc. These occurred at various times, and different stages, since nothing escaped Stanislavski's watchful eye, and they were incorporated into our exercises.

That is clear, I think, from the records of the *Tartuffe* rehearsals. In conclusion, I would only like to say a few words about one of the most important elements in an actor's technique: giving full physical expression to a role, characterising it externally. I dealt with this very little in my notes on rehearsals, because there was never an occasion when Stanislavski specially dwelt on it. He had his reasons, which were based on what he considered to be the most important aspects in our education. It would be a mistake, however, to consider that he attached secondary importance to it. He was a remarkable actor himself, a master of physical characterisation and, naturally, he led his pupils towards a similar mastery but, of course, in his own special way.

For him, acting is the art of experiencing and of physicalising. He absolutely forbade us to try and *act* feelings or the character. 'You must *behave* as the character,' he said. 'Of course, you can't behave without having feelings, but don't worry or think about them, they will emerge as the result of your concern with dynamic action within the given circumstances.'

Similarly, the search for physical characteristics should start with a deep understanding of the inner world of the character. Particular physical traits are more easily found when the character's whole logical line of behaviour has been absorbed and brought to life. The discovery of the inner 'kernel' of a character inevitably suggests the outer 'kernel'. A premature concern with the outside pushes an actor towards mere copying, and can be a barrier to the establishment of a living organic pattern of behaviour. External characterisation puts the finishing touches to an actor's work.

Did that mean that Stanislavski suggested we should repeat ourselves in every role, use our favourite habits, and reduce a role to our own limitations? Obviously not. When an actor solves the problem of how to give physical form to a character's sequence of actions, he starts with himself, his own natural qualities, and develops them creatively as he works. He must try to broaden them, and raise them to the level the play demands, or whatever the imagination of the people creating the production – the actors and the directors – has conceived.

Stanislavski tried every way he knew to protect us from the cheap methods of working on physical characterisation that were still current in the theatre, and which were based on a desire to cover a living face from the very outset with a mask that was put together out of a tired collection of 'typical' traits: lisping, stammering, altering one's natural voice, taking off one's pince-nez (a doctor) or twiddling one's moustache (an army officer), etc., etc., briefly, everything that encourages an actor to cling to what he finds easiest and most familiar, an external expression of character, which leads not to a fully rounded performance, but only to 'acting' its outer shell, its characteristics, and to 'acting' the character itself. Stanislavski, I repeat, considered this harmful. It prevented the development of a living person, or even killed it.

Of course, as an actor masters the logical sequence of the character's behaviour, his actions, and makes it run smoothly, he is, at the same time, spontaneously, perhaps unconsciously, discovering outer characteristics. That is inevitable. No matter how hard he tries at the beginning to avoid externals, to concentrate on what is of prime importance, his external appearance will appear in his imagination and from time to time, and one way or another, remind him of what it is. There's nothing to be afraid of here. Everything that emerges naturally, without force, during rehearsal should be gratefully accepted and used.

Stanislavski did not exclude the possibility, or the necessity, of directly looking for outer characteristics in a comparatively early phase of rehearsal. But again, he found his own way of doing it, and denied the actor any opportunity for mere copying. You only have to recall the rehearsal of *Tartuffe* when Kedrov found a way of astonishing Orgon. Isn't that a search for Tartuffe's particular external characteristics? Undeniably so. But this sudden moment of discovery was the discovery of a way to accomplish dynamic action, to astonish Orgon. It was the same in other cases.

In the final phases of rehearsal, the question of the external appearance of a role is of prime importance, but the answer must stem from and be the logical conclusion to everything that has gone before.

Stanislavski once had a conversation with me after he had seen a dress rehearsal of Dickens's *Pickwick Papers*, directed by Stanitsyn. I was playing Pickwick's manservant, Sam Weller. We talked on the telephone and I recall it from memory.

Stanislavski said:

'The externals are all very good. You're young, very agile, you move well but do you know what the purpose is? Agility for agility's sake? That's for the circus. Your actions aren't definite enough, they're not united by a common aim, they are sometimes contradictory, at others superfluous. The inner "kernel" of your character hasn't matured. That is what will unite all your moves and actions and make you believe in what you are doing.'

'What might be the kernel in this role?'

'That needs thinking about. It's difficult to give a quick answer. Perhaps being a nanny to Pickwick? So try to make everything you do serve one single end, to look after Pickwick and tend to his needs . . . Select what you need for that purpose and, however good it might have been in itself, get rid of the rest. Then the character becomes dynamic, it has something to aim for. That's the inner line. The outer "kernel", perhaps, if you have made him so agile and sharp, can be an acrobat or a monkey or something of that kind, whatever you find most exciting . . .'

When one of the greatest actors in the Russian theatre, Davydov, was talking to his pupils he regularly repeated:

'Above all, discover the trunk of a role, then its bigger branches, then the twigs and the shoots and the leaves and, finally, the veins in the leaves.'

Stanislavski, equally, saw the way to create a character as a definite sequence, as laying down a line of actions and making it strong. That came first and the rest, including outer form, after. But, of course, each of the various elements in a role implies the others: as an actor constructs the pattern of physical actions in the first phase of his work, he is, to a certain extent, already looking for particular characteristics. You can't have one without the other. But it is important for him not to think about it yet. When the moment came to start working on the outer characteristics of a role, its appearance, then Stanislavski did talk about it. However, when he asked an actor to change this or that characteristic, he proceeded extremely cautiously, gradually, trying not to present him with impossible tasks but, rather, helping him develop logically, in every single detail.

'What is a fat man? How does his behaviour differ from a thin man's? A fat man's body always leans backwards, his legs are bandy. Why is that? The centre of gravity in a stout man has shifted to his belly and that makes him lean backwards to maintain his balance, and his thick, fat thighs don't allow him to place his legs like a normal man. Hence the change in his way of walking.'

Making such remarks, Stanislavski would ask an actor to walk around the room with his legs wide apart and to imagine his stomach was heavier. He would then try to introduce this new characteristic first into one scene, then another, until the actor was completely at home with it. It was alive, organic and even the audience would believe he was fat, without any padding. So when he puts the padding on, it will be a natural part of his body and not foreign to it.

'What is an old man? Mainly his joints are stiff. He can't sit, stand without leaning his hands on something. That's the first thing you have to learn. The logic of a drunken man's behaviour is not that he staggers, but that he tries not to stagger. Find out how that is done.'

Analysing all the outer characteristics in this way showed the actor the way to master them and suggested the appropriate exercises. You only have to remember the exercise with a drop of mercury on the head, which he gave me during one of the *Dead Souls* rehearsals when I was playing Chichikov.

Is this strictly logical approach to a character really a cast-iron law or can there be other methods? Can't an actor, when he reads through his part, have an immediate picture of what the character looks like, or of individual features, and start by embodying them and so achieve the same result – a fully rounded complex figure? Of course, that can't be excluded. Several actors have spoken about this, as did Stanislavski in *My Life in Art*. Nonetheless, we have to take into account his experience as a director and an actor over many years, which told him that going from the inside to the outside is safer, more organic, and closer to our method of acting, which is designed to reflect the inner life of a character, rather that copy its external features. To doubt the efficacy of this aspect of Stanislavski's method is to doubt his method as a whole. We must not forget that Stanislavski proposed his method as something to use 'when it isn't working'. If it does work, using another method or no method at all, we have to consider that as an exception and allow that great artists work in any way they find necessary.

When I recall my own career – now forty years long – and consciously separate my successes from my failures, I have to state that the path Stanislavski showed me, even before I met him, when I was stumbling and groping my way along it, always suited me as an artist. Any deviation from this path invariably led to failure and disappointment.

First Presentation of Tartuffe *to the Management and Directors of the Moscow Art Theatre*

In 1938, after Stanislavski's death, an orphaned group of actors who had been working on *Tartuffe* were in a dubious situation. For many reasons, it seemed impossible to continue our experimental work without Stanislavski, but to stop would be a shame. The only proper answer seemed to be to complete the work we had begun by staging a production. But the management of the theatre had no idea whether we were ready or not. I couldn't tell myself. Stanislavski's work was so different from the usually accepted norm, that it was difficult to decide whether we had reached the point when we could responsibly stage anything.

We knew we had done a great deal of work, that we had drilled ourselves, that we had been successful here and there, that we knew the play and our own individual roles well. We could even perform one or two scenes, but we didn't know whether they were any good or not. All we knew was whether we had played a scene truthfully or falsely according to the 'notes' we had established for it. We hadn't yet played a single act right through, hadn't rehearsed all the scenes, and hadn't even touched the last act. Our mood was far from optimistic. In the theatre they clearly didn't believe we could perform *Tartuffe* successfully to an audience.

In the absence of any definite opinion on our part, the management of the theatre and the directors decided to see what we had done and then decide the fate of our production.

We needed time and a space for rehearsal. We had to put one or two acts together to show to the artistic director (Sakhnovski) and members of the board. From that moment our work came alive again. Molière's play appeared in the rehearsal schedule and we threw ourselves into our work. That now took a more practical character. We had to pull the individual bits together, introduce some order, remove the scaffolding to reveal at least some part of our intended building. We worked with energy and enthusiasm. We wanted to do our utmost so as not to disgrace the name of our teacher, and if we set aside a few disagreements, which are unavoidable in a creative group, we could say that our work was friendly.

We appeared at the presentation without the slightest inkling whether we would succeed or not. In his parting advice, Kedrov, who was now sole leader of our group, merely told us not to try too hard, not to 'do any "acting"'.

'No feelings, no flamboyance, just be sure of your actions,' he said.

The results of our presentation surpassed our expectations.

The first moves, the first lines, when no one was doing any 'acting', only 'adapting to each other', 'forming up with each other', produced great concentration in the audience, and that couldn't but be reflected in the way the actors felt. We came together even more, and concentrated more. Everything that had become normal and commonplace for us, so that we no longer even noticed it, the technique we had evidently in some measure acquired, appeared new, fresh and unexpected for those watching us. It aroused their interest, captured their attention and the more our concentration on the events of the play grew, the more they gripped us, the more they, too, were caught up in the turbulence of the family quarrel in Orgon's house. The consistency and logic of our actions produced a sense of belief, and released our energy and dynamism. The actors were unrecognisable. Their gifts were revealed as something different, unusual, they flowered unexpectedly. Everything we had done over such a long period, all Stanislavski and Kedrov's laborious, unending work, which we did not fully understand, and the fruits of which we had for so long been unaware, suddenly brought us unexpected results. Watching my friends acting, I was amazed at the ease with which they passed without thinking from one task to another, fulfilling them cleanly, convincingly, as though they had never experienced any difficulties or doubts, as though there had never been any blood, sweat and tears during rehearsals. I can't say anything about my own performance, except that in the scene with Cléante, when I tried to convince him of Tartuffe's saintliness, I really understood for the first time the meaning of, the profound significance in acting, what Stanislavski defined as 'inner images'. In that rehearsal, for the first time, I clearly visualised my meeting with Tartuffe when he was praying in church, how he wept over the flea and what his overall appearance was. I suddenly felt a passionate desire to convey all this clearly to Cléante (played by Geirot) and was annoyed: why couldn't he understand? I could see he didn't from the expression in his eyes, the sceptical corners of his mouth that were pulled down, ready to break into a sarcastic smile any moment, his shoulders drawn back with impatience, etc., etc. I didn't miss a single sign of tacit resistance. I read all his thoughts, and each one of them poured oil on the fire. I repeat, I can't say whether I acted well or not, but certainly all these elements were undoubtedly present in the scene with Cléante and when at the end of the scene Geirot told me he had seen for the first time how unexpectedly alive, how 'eloquent' my eyes were, I understood that in this rehearsal he too had mastered the same technique. We realised that each of us had risen above the difficulties that had seemed insurmountable the day before.

The presentation was a triumph. We had successfully completed the first phase of our work. Opinions about us changed, conversations in the corridors now took a different tack. The next day, Sakhnovski, the theatre's artistic director, had a long discussion with his fellow directors. Kedrov, Bogovlenskaya and I were also present. Sakhnovski was surprised by the 'new kind' of acting.

'I never thought that this comedy by Molière, or, indeed, any of his plays could be performed so convincingly, that it would have a living quality. I believed that everyone who entered really came into a room, not "from the wings", and on a matter of great personal importance. You were all bound together by a thousand family ties. I believed that Elmire was really Orgon's wife, and Marianne, his daughter, and not just simply actors and actresses playing parts. In short, I believed from beginning to end that this was real life, I understood the passion with which the members of the family defended their home, I felt for them. I couldn't remain indifferent to the progress of this struggle, and felt ready at any moment to take part in it, although I virtually know the play by heart. I was so excited, so shaken! You spared me the typical, traditional Molière production, known across the world. The remarkable feature of your performance is that you kept the connection between the lives of the characters and your own, you brought your own genuine living feelings to them and discarded all the tired old clichés so familiar in Molière. I'm only afraid that they may creep into your performance later when you put on the wigs and costumes of the period.'

Words cannot express the satisfaction such an appreciation of our work gave us. It meant that we had, to some extent, achieved the kind of acting Stanislavski had led us towards. It only remained to hold on to what we had achieved and to develop it further into a complete performance of Molière's play.

Kedrov undertook this mission, and tried to resolve other problems that arose from the change in our intentions. If the preceding period can be called work on technique, on the re-education of the actor and the acquisition of a new method of working on oneself, now we had to create a finished production on the basis of what we had learned, which would be a synthesis of all the elements of theatre. It is not a play about ingenious stock characters but about great passions, a comedy with stark situations when feelings run intensely high. Although it was three hundred years old, we wanted to bring *Tartuffe* alive again as a passionate, contemporary play, so that in our time, as in Molière's, it would angrily, powerfully expose hypocrisy and put an end to sanctimonious humbug. Stanislavski had laid the foundations for it and after considerable work, Kedrov staged *Tartuffe* on 4 December 1939.[1] The following epigraph appeared on the posters and in the programme:

> *This work was begun under the direction of*
> *People's Artist K.S. Stanislavski*
> *and is dedicated to his memory.*

[1] Fifteen months after Stanislavski's death.

In one of his statements about *Tartuffe*, Kedrov said:

'When we created this production, we used the method of physical action. What is this method? Stanislavski said that when we talk about "physical actions" we mislead the actor. They are psychophysical actions, but we call them physical to avoid unnecessary discussion, because physical actions are real, they can be set. The precision of an action, its concrete fulfilment in any given production is the basis of our kind of acting. If I know an action, its logic, precisely, that, for me, is like a musical score. The way I perform it, here, today, now, for a particular audience, is a creative moment, but I still have the score.'

Using his work on *Tartuffe*, Stanislavski offered a multifaceted, forward-looking education for the actor, and Kedrov, who completed his work, created a performance in which human voices were heard. Usually Molière is presented as a display of acting. A display for its own sake. It always has the coldness of a firework display, where trick follows trick in the name of being 'theatrical'. This cheap vulgarity disappeared at the Moscow Art Theatre, people were revealed in all their human truth, leading the actors to the highest form of theatricality. Therein lies, I think, the significance of the Moscow Art Theatre production, its principle.

The production had an obvious success with audiences. The critics were also enthusiastic and we were especially pleased that they noted the qualities we had striven for. For my own part, I can't make any judgement on the results we achieved, as I was in the thick of everything, and could not see anything from the outside.

One thing was certain for the company of *Tartuffe* – the presence of a creative atmosphere both on and off stage during performances. I'm not just talking about the actors, who both understood and felt the heavy responsibility they bore. All the backstage staff, to whom Kedrov gave a special talk, also understood the significance of this show and worked creatively on it.

We felt the invisible presence of Stanislavski among us and our super-supertask was the desire not to disgrace his memory.

Conclusion

'The more I think about acting,' Stanislavski once said, 'the shorter my definition of good acting becomes. If you ask me how I define it, my answer is: "It is the kind of acting in which there is a SUPERTASK and a THROUGH-ACTION. Bad acting is when there is neither." '

The major demand Stanislavski made on art was that it should contain ideas. But he never considered giving living form to the idea of a dramatic work by cold, run-of-the-mill technique. He dreamed of a technique that could deal with genuine, human feelings and speak of genuine, human experiences and passions.

'Playing a part means taking the life of the human spirit on to the stage,' Stanislavski said. 'Can you do that if you don't really create the flowing stream of human life? Of course, the mere fact that what happens on stage is organic doesn't create a dramatic work of art. But by establishing an organic pattern, by selecting what is necessary, and rejecting what is unnecessary or superfluous, the actor or the director makes the stream of dramatic life convincing and gives it meaning and purpose, and so creates the qualities which are the hallmarks, the characteristic truths of a work of art, and they will be qualitatively higher the more organic the pattern is, and our imaginary life will be closer to real life.'

He was far from satisfied with the contemporary state of acting, and often said: 'Our acting is still amateur, because we have no theory. We don't know its laws, we don't even know the elements of which it is composed. Take music, for example. It has a precise theory and a musician has everything he needs at his disposal to develop his technique. He has innumerable exercises and studies to train the skills he needs as an artist: nimble fingers, a developed sense of rhythm, a good ear, bowing technique etc., etc. He knows perfectly well that the basic element in his art is *sound*. He knows the sound of the scales he uses, he knows, in brief, what he must do to achieve perfection, and there isn't a single violinist, even a modest member of the second violins who, apart from playing in concerts, doesn't practise four or five hours a day. And it is the same in the other arts. But show me one actor who does anything to perfect his technique outside of performance and rehearsal. You can't, he doesn't exist, for the simple reason it is acting, he wouldn't know where to begin. We don't know the basic elements of our own art. We don't have any scales, we don't have any studies or exercises, we don't know how to train and develop our talent. And the amazing thing is that nobody cares. Indeed, this is seen as the special charm of our art, in that its future development depends not on some kind of irksome theory, akin to mathematics, but entirely on "inspiration".'

Stanislavski, who had scaled the heights in his creative work as a director and an actor, was also remarkable in that he made a proper study of its basic laws. He created a method which opened up limitless possibilities for improving an actor's technique, for personal growth and development, and so for growth and progress in the theatre as a whole.

When he was watching great actors at work, he tried to understand, to isolate the special features that made their acting really great art, the means by which this was achieved, which method they used when working on a role, what their overall artistic process was, what their artistic personality was, and whether it was possible once the elements of acting had been defined, to create a technique by which ordinary actors, through hard work and daily training, could overcome their limitations more easily, and perfect and refine their technique. That was the truest, shortest way to an actor's natural creative personality.

Stanislavski's work with actors was a process of removing blocks to their creative abilities.

Stock-in-trade acting only has one or two, at most ten, methods of dealing with a dramatic moment, but nature has an infinite number of methods. So, don't force her, obey her laws. That is the only proper way. Regular work on yourself to perfect your technique will bring you into accord with nature. Truth and belief are the path to organic creativity. We have to create a normal stream of events on stage so as to set our organism and the subconscious to work.

It is difficult to see how any art can develop theory or technique, when its constituent elements are unknown. The elements of any art form must be clearer than clear. Who can doubt that in music it is sounds, in painting it is colours, in drawing, line, in mime, gesture, and in literature and poetry, words. But in acting? . . . Ask a few people in the theatre and they will all give you a different answer; as a rule, it will not be the one that was accepted as incontrovertible truth a thousand years ago. The main element in acting is *action*, 'genuine, organic, productive, appropriate action', as Stanislavski used to stress.

A character in a play is above all a man in action. The actor is called upon to give flesh and blood to the dramatic sequence of a character's actions as written. He divides the play up into episodes, he defines the logic of the individual links of what will be the unbroken chain of the conflict. That is how work on a role begins. Defining the 'tasks', the 'through-action', the 'kernel' of a role are not things that can be done quickly but are the result of long questioning, and we start by deciding on the simplest, most self-evident 'tasks'. As he passes from one episode to another, the actor begins to see clearly his whole line of behaviour, his conflict and its logical development throughout the play. This line must be continuous in the actor's mind. It starts long before the play begins, and ends after the final curtain. It must be continuous, too, when he is not on stage. It must be given clean, clear embodiment, with no unnecessary doubts, and it must be completely truthful and organic. When, in real life, someone is trying to make a reputation and create confidence in those around him, he has to be circumspect in his actions, and must never disrupt their logic and sequence but accomplish them truthfully.

An actor's ability to be convincing is based on these rules. Establishing the logical sequence of a character's behaviour, then making it vital and organic as you embody it, is the basis on which a fully rounded character is created. And so an actor's work must begin with a search for this sequence and its 'organic nature'. This is the correct, or rather, the only naturally correct way. To give living form to any action means you have to summon up all the elements that constitute human behaviour. In life, this happens unconsciously, as a natural reaction to some kind of external event; on stage all events are imaginary, and cannot, therefore, provoke a natural reaction. How can we achieve an organic sequence of behaviour in a character in a play?

Stanislavski drew our attention to what is most tangible, most concrete in any human action: its physical aspect. In his directing and teaching, especially in his final years, he laid the greatest significance on this aspect of the life of a role when organising the beginning of work. Splitting off the physical aspect of human behaviour from its other elements is, of course, artificial, but he used it as a teaching strategy. By diverting actors' attention away from feelings and the psychological, and directing them towards the fulfilment of 'purely physical' actions, he helped them gain access to their feelings in an organic, natural manner as they performed them.

'Build the simplest possible pattern of physical actions,' said Stanislavski. 'Follow it in an unbroken line and you have mastered thirty-five per cent of the role already.'

The pattern of physical actions is the bare bones on to which all the essentials of a human character can be grafted. It is also a method of testing whether our behaviour on stage is organic and the most expressive reflexion of the feelings a character experiences and everything about him.

The technical expertise Stanislavski called for rarely comes easily. It can be achieved by a great deal of hard work and daily exercises throughout one's life. To imagine that one can occupy a place in the ranks of those geniuses to whom all is given as a 'gift from heaven' is a nonsense. A genius is a rare occurrence, and it is much better to tell yourself, once and for all, that acting is difficult, and what is difficult can only be overcome by persistence and application. Unfortunately, there are few who understand this, because acting seems simple and easy from the outside. And the more accomplished an actor's work is the simpler and easier it appears.

An actor who possesses a fully developed technique, enabling him to create living, convincing human characters, has the right to occupy the place of honour which our country affords a genuine artist. His art is profound, subtle, it makes its mark and reaches audiences. They are grateful to him for one moment of uplifting emotion, they take this feeling home with them and their lives are affected by the performance. We can only feel deep respect for such an actor who has mastered the art of truth and we must recognise the power he has over our hearts.

If you want to create truth on stage, you must develop an awareness of it. It is like a musician's ear. The ability is, to a greater or lesser extent, innate but it can also be developed. Theatrical truth and organic behaviour require the actor constantly to work on himself throughout his career, to study life and his own times. He must also study thoroughly all the most subtle nuances out of which human relationships are woven, the way they are expressed in often barely perceptible, almost invisible physical actions, and include them in his daily exercises. We must do things that we do easily, unconsciously in life, consciously again and then make them easy, unconscious, habitual on stage. Stanislavski gave his pupils a whole range of exercises for that purpose.

Many of our leading figures in the theatre – including managers and critics – have often stood up against the technique Stanislavski proposed. They label it as 'mathematics', 'precision engineering', etc. This is only because merely a few have made a practical study of new techniques and few, therefore, understand them. Studying them presents great difficulties. But the director who is called upon, with the actors, to stage a dramatic work, and the actor, through whom the director conveys the dramatist's idea to the audience, do not have the right to ignore any opportunity to develop their technique, however difficult it may appear at first. Directors and actors who do not have this technique and at the same time are not happy with the usual, run-of-the-mill methods in the theatre, try to find new means of expression either through conscious stylisation or by replacing acting with anything that happens to be to hand, and are then convinced that they have revealed new ways of acting. That is a total delusion! A theatrical performance, which is basically a mirror of human life, can only carry conviction when it is expressed in living, organic actions. The ability to create genuine, living, artistic characters is the particular good fortune of the actor's art, and there is no sense in rejecting this golden opportunity, and, in so doing, impoverishing that art. But creating living human figures requires, I repeat, a very special kind of mastery, a special technique. It is quite different from what is often understood by those terms. That is no more than a routine facsimile of art. These two techniques are different from each other, in the way real plants in a nursery differ from artificial flowers made in a factory.

Not infrequently, some actors, who do not have a reputation for subtlety – rather the opposite – are described as having a wonderful technique. It is usually said about them: 'Yes, they are tasteless, crude, but they have a wide-ranging technique.' Technique that produces crude, tasteless acting is not technique at all, or rather, not the kind of technique we are talking about. The capacity to impress an unsophisticated audience with well-tried, cheap effects, agility, to 'give' a funny line or sentimental aphorism with clear diction, to get a round of applause, to make showy entrances and exits, to get big curtain calls at the end of the show, to upstage the other actors and drown their lines or use them cleverly to make their success your own, etc., etc., is just a collection of stock industrial skills. They can be crude, as I have said, or more subtle when a more demanding audience sees their skills at work but they cannot essentially be regarded as what Stanislavski called artistic technique and so are of no interest to us.

So, great acting demands characters who are genuine, living people. The actor who succeeds from time to time in creating a fusion between the character in the play and himself undoubtedly feels something important has occurred and experiences artistic pleasure. This doesn't happen very often and so, once having felt it, actors are always dissatisfied with any kind of surrogate in their work, even when a routine performance is successful with the audience. No, only when an actor has genuinely lived the life of a character he has created in his imagination, and when the logic of that being has become his logic, and the actions which this logic dictates are performed in all their subtlety by the obedient, living organs of the actor/person, when all the subtle experiences and the events his brain has conceived have been absorbed into his own nervous system, does he begin to feel the joy of a master who has created a genuine work of art.

Rooting himself in the great traditions of the Russian theatre, studying the techniques of acting and directing, Stanislavski achieved results that were unprecedented in the history of world theatre. His gigantic step forward in developing and strengthening politically committed realism – which has always distinguished our national theatre – as a forward-looking force, and in arming actors with a progressive technique, which helps them attain this goal, is, indeed, an invaluable service to the theatre, and we must praise a genius of the Soviet fatherland.

The great socialist October Revolution opened up such limitless opportunities for Stanislavski's creative experiments as we can only dream of. It enabled this great theatrical master to complete the studies he had pursued all his life, brilliantly.

Stanislavski's legacy must be studied thoroughly and mastered as the most perfect weapon in our struggle for great ideas on the cultural front.